T0286902

What If YOU Are the Answer?

ALSO BY RACHEL HOLLIS

Girl, Wash Your Face

Girl, Stop Apologizing

Didn't See That Coming

What If YOU Are the Answer?

And 26 Other Questions That Just Might Change Your Life

Rachel Hollis

Authors Equity
1123 Broadway, Suite 1008
New York, New York 10010

Cover design by Chris Sergio
Cover photograph © Melanie Dunea
Book design by Scribe Inc.

Most Authors Equity books are available at a discount when purchased in quantity for sales promotions or corporate use. Special editions, which include personalized covers, excerpts, and corporate imprints, can be created when purchased in large quantities. For more information, please email info@authorsequity.com.

Library of Congress Control Number: 2024947628
Print ISBN 9798893310177
Ebook ISBN 9798893310405

Printed in the United States of America
Second Printing

www.authorsequity.com

For Cez

Contents

Good questions are powerful.

As powerful as the moon controlling oceans from two hundred thousand miles away and turning perfectly upstanding citizens into werewolves against their will. Good questions are influential. As compelling as Julia Roberts's crying in a movie—why do I *immediately* start crying too?

Good questions are like that—they force the point.

At least they do with me.

Sometimes good questions knock me sideways with a perspective I've never seen before. Sometimes they work their way into the deep crevices of my mind, a surprise to unearth later—a forgotten piece of hard candy at the bottom of grandma's purse. Good questions won't let go until I've given them time and attention. Good questions can be a catalyst for change, directions at a crossroads, or the swift kick in the butt we need to push us out of our comfort zone.

Six years ago, someone asked me a good question, and it changed the course of my life. *If you could write a book about anything at all, and readers would actually retain what you share, what would you tell them?*

Before the prompt, I hadn't even known I had an answer to that question. It must have been bubbling in my subconscious along with the dialogue to any Disney movie made before 1998 because just like *The Lion King* soundtrack, when prompted, it all came spilling out of me.

What would I share with people if I could share anything? The hard truths and life lessons it had taken me decades to learn. I wrote the book I wish I could have read when I was twenty-five. I wrote a love letter to imaginary readers, the kind of things I wished someone would have said to me.

Like, no matter how small you sometimes feel, you are powerful beyond measure. I shared what Epictetus said, that we can't control what happens to us in life, but we *can* control our response to it.

Ancient Stoics knew what was up.

I wrote about surviving pain and trauma, how it can weaken us—make us bitter or terrified or mean. But it can also make us the strongest kind of warrior, able to lead ourselves and others with compassion and grit. I wrote about hardship and how the single determining factor in who you become on the other side of it is the meaning you place on the experience.

I was so passionate about sharing all I had learned that I'd written the first chapter of what would later become *Girl, Wash Your Face* within the hour.

I remember someone telling me, "Enjoy this process. You'll likely only ever have enough ideas for one book like this." As if at thirty-four, I'd acquired all the wisdom I ever would.

Back when I wrote that first personal development book, I was so excited to share every idea that I thought might be helpful. *Do this, or try that, or consider this . . . here are three different things that helped me, and maybe they'll help you too!* I'm so proud of those pages and the two self-work books that have followed it up. I'm proud that people have gotten something out of lines I wrote and still fairly shocked that anyone listens to my thoughts on the regular. But in the last eight years, you know what I've learned?

I don't actually know anything.

Or really, I suppose that's not accurate.

I know lots of things. I'm a veritable treasure trove of ideas for self-improvement and random bits of pop trivia and historical facts and lines from movies and the lyrics to just about every song I've ever heard, especially jingles from radio commercials for small local businesses from my childhood. *Marine parts are so easy to buy . . . at Galey's Marine Supply. Toot Toot.* That one has lived rent-free in my brain for thirty-five years.

But what I don't know are *the answers that will be most helpful for* ***you***.

The capital-*T* truths I believe today with all my might? Time has taught me that they might potentially be swept away at a moment's notice.

I wrote the chapters of this book, in no particular order, over four of the most challenging years of my life. I wrote through disillusionment and divorce. I wrote while my business, built around live events, burned down in the pandemic. I wrote while navigating new love. I wrote while recovering from a miscarriage. I wrote while parenting my four children through the grief of losing their father. I wrote while moving back across the country, starting where we once began, a fresh chapter after so many years of absolute shit.

"Everyone has a plan until they get punched in the face."

Mike Tyson, the prophet.

Life has punched me—and I'm sure you too—in the face *many* times, and in those moments of shock that immediately follow something hard or the months (*OK, but really, it's years*) of overthinking I do in the aftermath, I often have a prospective shift about whole parts of my worldview. What I've learned is that, at any moment, I'm one life experience away from having a totally different belief about how the world works. All I know—*all any of us can ever know*—is what's real and true for us, in this moment, today.

But I had no idea that was the case when I began my self-work. How could I? When you're starting to work on any part of your life for the first time (health, mental well-being, business, relationships), it's pretty damn scary.

Chances are you weren't raised with a ton of resources or guides. You likely don't have a lot of tools for emotional evolution in your toolbox, which is why you start looking for help. In the beginning, you're not working on yourself because you're great at it. I wish! You're working on yourself because you've experienced a catalyst of such acute pain, you vowed you'd never find yourself there again. In those moments, we don't even know where the hell we're going—we just know we don't want to be where we are.

Enter: someone with ideas!

No, not ideas. They've got *answers*.

And they've got the charisma to propose those answers to you in a way that changes your whole perspective. Now you have a guide to help you down the road you started walking without any clear indication of where the path leads. This can be wildly supportive when you're starting out. Nobody knows what they're doing when they're new to it, so it helps to have someone there gently reminding us what to do next. Like when you're little, and you finally start using the toilet on your own, and every time you go, some older, wiser person has to remind you, *Hey, buddy, great job. Don't forget to wipe your butt.*

Sage advice.

But just like with wiping your butt, if you're truly evolving, then the guidance you start *any* journey with will have a natural plateau. The excitement and energy you had at the beginning of the marathon will be long gone when you're at mile twenty-two and there's no gas left in your tank. The swagger you possess as a small business owner with your first customer is MIA three years later when the economy is in a nosedive and you're not sure how you'll make payroll. The euphoria you experience as a first-time parent holding your newborn to your chest is hard to tap into when you're trying to calm a **three**nager in a temper tantrum or a fifteen-year-old who's struggling with anxiety.

As our lives change, as the journey takes new twists and turns on the trail, we need new skills, new knowledge, and new perspectives.

And that's where I find myself . . . both as a student of life and as a sharer of ideas.

Once upon a time, I thought I needed to have all the answers, both for myself and for anyone who might read what I wrote or listen to me speak or watch something I create. But the older I get, the more I understand that if you're looking to someone else for *your* answers, you run the risk of getting a watered-down version of a truth that only applies to you in *some areas*. Worse still, we'll raise up subsequent generations without the ability to think critically, utilize common sense, and hold space for the magic and mystery of a universe so vast, we'll never be able to understand it all.

And if we'll never be able to understand it all, why would we assume we can ever really, truly have capital-*T* truths about any of it?

So, my friend, I'm no longer looking for answers; I'm looking for wisdom.

I'm collecting stories and ideas and thoughts and experiences like a little girl catching fireflies, and I'm doing it with a similar sense of wonder.

My core value in life is growth, and I spent the early part of my adulthood believing that growth looked like rising up. But now I think growth might actually be growing out.

And down.

And sideways.

Growth is a stretch in every direction—even directions you didn't know existed.

That kind of growth happens when we learn, yes, from others, but most especially when we learn *ourselves*. The single greatest thing I can do in this life and with this work is not try to teach you what I think is true but potentially to ask you questions that help you discover your own truth.

And so this isn't a book of answers *because only you have those*; this is a book of questions.

Because the right question can change everything.

That's what questions do . . . they teach us about ourselves, they make us think, and if we're honest in the reply, questions have the ability to give us our own answers.

That's my intention with this work. It's a collection of questions that I've learned to ask myself—a firefly in my jar. Might I suggest that as you read each chapter, you sit with the question for a moment (or a week?) before you ever read my take on it? After all, it doesn't really matter what I think about it; it only matters what ***you*** think about it. The answers to these questions have had such a profound effect on my life that it changed something for me instantly. I hope these questions, and the pondering they produce, might have a profound effect on you too.

But if not, that's OK. We've established that I may not really know anything. I've just got some ideas that have been real and true and good for me . . . at least until I get punched in the face again.

xo, Rach

What If YOU Are the Answer?

~~What~~ *Who* are you waiting for?

I'm not going to tell you what to do in this book. I swear I'm not. But if—hypothetically—I *was* going to offer you any advice, it would be this: **Live Your Life.**

I know. It sounds as basic and as obvious as the "Live, Laugh, Love" sign your mom got on clearance at TJ Maxx, but this edict is actually surprisingly complex, and very few people truly pull it off. Let's break it down.

Live: If you ask one hundred people what it means to really live, you'll get one hundred different answers. If you ask me, there is only one. To me, *living* means that we actively take part in the creation of the world we exist inside of. It means we become truly conscious that we're *not* an NPC in someone else's video game. *You* are the main character of *your* life, and truly living means *you act like it*!

Don't believe me?

Scream. Scream right now at the top of your lungs. Or don't, because that would be weird ... but just imagine if you *did scream*. How would the energy in the room shift? If you're on an airplane, you're gonna cause some trouble—an air marshal will probably be called, and you'll have to explain yourself. If you're in a coffee shop, maybe you get some looks, maybe some people will leave

(I definitely would). If you're all alone, then at the very least, the scream probably woke you up and made your heart pump to a faster rhythm. Those are just a few possible outcomes for your scream—we didn't even touch on how the outcomes differ when you adjust the variables.

How you scream can change everything too: *blood curdling, banshee, battle cry, samurai, little kid scared of bees, gale force winds through the trees, I scream, ice cream . . . all depends on how you scream.*

And then there's **what**.

What you scream adds in new elements:

Narwhals are the unicorns of the sea!
One hundred million dollars?!
Someone's poisoned the water hole!
Carl, you pestilent whoreson!

Try out any of those screams without warning—and as loudly as possible—and you're going to get completely different responses.

See, at any moment, with the smallest amount of effort, you can change the energy of the world around you. Screaming in public is obnoxious, yes, and chances are you're not gonna do it for all the same reasons *I'm not gonna do it* . . . my point is, though, ***we could***.

We could also quit our jobs and move to Peru.

We could finally learn to play the guitar or take up tap dancing or invest our life savings in an alpaca farm . . . I'm not saying we're gonna do it—*but we could*.

Living life means getting the most out of it that we can. And not in some greedy, selfish, consumeristic kind of way—but in a soak-up-the-goodness-all-around-you, embrace-the-hard-stuff-too, fill-and-feel-all-the-way-to-the-edges-of-each-day kind of way. But if you're repeating the same patterns day after day, seeing the same people, eating the same food, telling yourself the same stories, the monotony isn't a routine—it's the death knell.

To live means that *you know* that you are in the driver's seat. Being in the driver's seat doesn't require you to go one hundred miles an hour . . . or anywhere at all. But living means every day you remain conscious of your ability to change direction and create a different life, different day, or even just a different experience in the next sixty seconds.

There's a brilliant idea in Seth Godin's *The Dip*, and I haven't stopped thinking about it since I read it years ago. The whole book is about what to do when something important in your life has become monotonous.

In the book, Seth asks, *What do you do when your life, relationship, career, model-train-building hobby goes stagnant or "dips"?* Turns out, most people make the wrong choice when they're confused about what the right path might be. When we try to decide if we should give up on the thing that's lost its magic and momentum, most people make a decision to either quit or keep going, hoping things will get better. But—and this is the bit I'm obsessed with—"the opposite of quitting isn't just to keep going," Seth says. *"The opposite of quitting is recommitting with passion."*

Holy crap. It's so good, it hurts my feelings that I didn't think of that line first.

How many people just "keep going"? They think that if they get through the next week or the next month or get the kids launched off to college, *then* things will really start to feel better and fuller and more energized. But that's not how it works. If you want a life that feels better to you, *you* have to make it that way. Today. With passion.

Living means you don't simply exist; it means you actively *create* what's happening.

Your: Your life. Not your mama's life or *his mama's* life or your favorite influencer or your favorite saint.

Your life.

What do you like? What are you into? What do you think would be rad or magical or fun or outrageous?

Do you even know?

Because most of us walk a tightrope between the calling of our heart and what other people expect (and will accept) from us. When the fear of judgment is so deeply ingrained, it's possible you've never even considered what you like or who you really are. You've maybe never considered who you really are because you're so damn fantastic at being who everyone else thinks you should be.

Disregarding your true nature in order to be a more likable version for someone else is sneaky. We often don't actually realize it's occurred until we're deeply inside a life we just sort of went along with. I'm convinced this is actually what's happening when someone goes through a "midlife crisis." It starts with a dullness of spirit that catches us in quiet moments: *Is this all there is?* asks the voice in our head.

The quiet desperation in that single thought is so visceral, we shut it down immediately. Instead, we pour a glass of wine, or dream about the next vacation, or plan a remodel of the kitchen cabinets . . . or maybe we should just sell this house and move somewhere else?

Distractions, every single one.

Distract yourself or numb yourself or deny yourself—do *anything* other than face yourself. Distract yourself enough, and this whisper will get even quieter. Distract yourself enough, and you'll make it through your entire life a creation of someone else's opinions and your unwillingness to challenge the norm. I suppose in that scenario, you really are the NPC . . . the supporting character in your spouse's life story, or your parent's happy ending, or your mother-in-law's scripted drama.

What a goddamn waste that would be.

How about we *don't* do that?

How about you live *your* life—which means you spend every day that you're able to figuring out what *your* version of life actually is?

How about you try some new stuff and see if you dig it?

How about you learn to look at other humans as individual players in their own stories without feeling the need to write yours the same way?

How about you listen to your heart, your gut, your inner knowing—that still, small voice inside you that's constantly giving truth and wisdom?

That monologue will always shoot you straight. If only you'll listen, you'll hear it saying:

Yes.
No.
Not right now.
Dangerous.
Wonderful.
Worth trying.
Needs more salt.

How about you give yourself permission to get it wrong? How about you give yourself permission to change lanes, directions, occupations, beliefs, and other things you need to on the journey of trying your best to do your best? How about you try things out in little, tiny inches or huge, gigantic miles depending on what allows for the healthiest, most vibrant version of you? And how about you do all of those things in pursuit of the best life *you're* able to live?

Life: You know that classic quote / mantra / bumper sticker that says, "You only live once"? At some point in the last decade, a very wise person pointed out how inherently inaccurate this statement is.

You don't live once—you die once. You'll live (I hope) every single day from now until then. That's the thing about your life and my life and every life in between—the one thing they all share is that eventually, **they will end**. So as Mary Oliver asks us, "What is it you plan to do with your one wild and precious life?"

In the strict religious culture of my childhood, the focus was almost exclusively on the *afterlife*. The sermons and lessons I heard weekly from both my father and my grandfather (both fire-and-brimstone Pentecostal preachers) revolved around how you could live *this life* in such a way that you'd be guaranteed a beautiful existence after you died.

Sometimes when I write about the things I was taught growing up, I feel like I'm writing about an alien planet. This is one of those instances.

The idea that you would try to mold your <u>one single life</u> (a place you actually exist inside of) for the sole focus of checking enough boxes to get into heaven (a place you've only heard described) feels completely absurd to me. The idea that this life isn't as important as whatever comes after it is deeply flawed. It's an ideology that became a sort of numbing mechanism for so many people I grew up with. They'd find themselves in a hardship: troubled marriage, toxic work environment, financial struggles . . . and they'd repeat a mantra that was affirmed by everyone in their church family: "God has a plan."

They'd repeat this mantra while staying right where they were. They'd repeat it while carrying on at the same crappy job, with the same awful boss, year after year. They'd repeat it while their husband kept cheating. They'd repeat it while continuing to dig themselves into further debt.

God has a plan, they'd say.

You're damn right God has a plan, Becky—*but do you?*

Life is a joint collaboration. Life is a dance between you and something divine.

Do you have a plan to meet God halfway? Because there's ***no way*** that the only reason you're here is to live your life following a course map that somebody else created for you.

You will *never* convince me that the same source who created a trillion twinkling stars and white sandy beaches and underwater volcanoes and weenie-dog puppies and those vibrant tree frogs in the Amazon and a million other beautiful things—who created you and me and all that's majestic—put us on a giant magical spinning ball of dirt just so we could properly follow enough rules to get to *some other place.*

Did you know that there was a 1 in 400,000,000,000,000 chance of *you* even being born *you*? Seriously. Look it up. 1 in 400,000,000,000,000 were the odds that you'd even be here at all. Imagine for a moment that you were diagnosed with some rare form of cancer and they told you that you had a 1 in 400,000,000,000,000 chance at survival, and against **those** odds, *you lived.* I have a friend who beat a 30 percent chance of surviving cancer, and <u>everything about her changed</u>. Being told she was close to death only to find the strength to fight and live? It changed her approach to life, the abundance of her love for others, her presence in this moment, her use of time and energy, and even her willingness to splurge on the things she used to fear spending money on:

things like delicious dinners or tickets to the Philharmonic. And that was a 30 percent chance to live.

You and me and the weenie-dog puppies? We got a 1 in 400,000,000,000,000! But most of the population is sleepwalking through life believing it isn't special or precious.

You are both. You are extremely special and impossibly precious, and your unawareness of that fact is what allows you to treat this sacred opportunity that you've been given without intention.

Let's be intentional.

Let's realize that no one else can solve our problems, heal our wounds, or make the most of the opportunity we've been given. People can make your life fuller, better, and more beautiful—but no matter how wonderful they are, *they* aren't the ones who will make the most of this experience. It's on you. *You* are the hero you've been waiting for.

Don't waste the chance.

My life experience continues to remind me, in the most painful ways, that tomorrow isn't guaranteed. So don't miss the opportunity to live **your** life, and live it well.

What <u>**must**</u> you let go of?

At the beginning of each year, my friends and I used to host what we called a "Vision Cast." We'd gather at some aesthetically pleasing local coffeehouse, commandeer a large table, then spend half a day planning for the year ahead. We called it Vision Cast because we were laying out the high-level vision for our lives . . . and also because it sounded cool.

Sure, we could have planned our year out by ourselves, but having other people involved in our New Year's resolutions elevated our individual visions. It's way harder to sell yourself short when your hype squad believes you're worth a million bucks. But more than that, all those other people hearing about your goals generates collective accountability. After all, if Mary Sue told you on January 10 that she really dislikes her job and she's committed to finding a better place to work, it gives you full permission to challenge her on why she's still trapped there when she complains about it in June. Not everyone is a safe space for your life's vision; hopes and dreams are delicate little robin's eggs and very easily shattered. But if you have people you can trust, I don't know any better way to kick off a new year—especially if you enjoy deep conversation and espresso-based beverages.

Having the group's accountability throughout the year was

awesome, but having their insight during the actual Vision Cast? Vital. Everyone came to the table with an idea or a process that had helped them the previous year. Over the years, we tested out each person's ideas and frameworks and eventually distilled them down into a tried-and-true agenda we used again and again. The highlight of which were definitely the questions we each had to answer about the previous year in order to help us better prepare for the next one. The best of the best of these?

What ***must*** *you let go of in order to be the person you want to be?*

That *right there* is a *hellofa* question! Can we just sit with it for a minute?

If you know the answer to that question, it can change your whole life. That's some *get brutally freaking honest with ourselves about why we keep holding onto the same people, practices, and habits that are destroying our potential!*

That's a *badass* question right there.

But this badass question started as an anemic, awkward version of the move-maker she would become. Back in the beginning, at the early Vision Cast get-togethers, the question we *actually asked* was, ***What do you need to let go of?***

OK, sure, it's fine. It doesn't blow my hair back, but it's a good start for contemplation—particularly if you've never considered the idea before. But what we didn't understand when we first dreamed it up is that this question *doesn't require any real commitment*. If you're really, truly trying to change your life for the better, you MUST be willing to commit or you'll be saying the exact same stuff at Vision Cast again next year.

If you ask yourself, **What do I need to let go of?**

You can come up with all kinds of suitable answers:

I need to let go of my dependence on alcohol as a coping mechanism.
I need to let go of unfulfilling sex as a substitute for intimacy.
I need to let go of this debilitating obsession with my parents' approval.
I need to let go of those clothes and a fixation on a body I don't have anymore.
I need to stop this never-ending toxic relationship with my ex-girlfriend.
I need to let go of worry about what other people will think if I come out.

All of us can come up with things in our life that we know *shouldn't* be there—but the power of the badass question is that it doesn't ask what you *need* to let go of; it asks what ***you must let go*** *of and then it doubles down . . .* **in order to be the best version of yourself.**

Must isn't a possibility; it's a necessity. The "best version of ourselves" leaves little room for negotiation or excuses. By changing the *words* we use to ask ourselves questions, the questions become more compelling. The more compelling, the more likely they are to give us answers that will provoke—at the very least—a different perspective and, at most, lasting change.

This is powerful work at an annual get-together, a journaling session on your birthday, or a discussion topic at the top of a new year. But imagine—*ooh hoo hoo*, just imagine—how much your life might change for the better if you were to ask this question of yourself every single month!

And *this*, friends, is how our annual Vision Cast morphed into the monthly Full Moon Dinner. We realized a year was too long to go in between check-ins. We wanted something more consistent, a regular way to touch base, see where we were and how closely our paths resembled the ones we said we wanted to be walking.

A monthly check-in seemed much more effective.

It was a great way to acknowledge the passing of each month, and frankly, I love any reason to celebrate, *especially if it feels sort of witchy.*

Why do it on a full moon? Better question: why not? A little research revealed that the full moon represents the completion of a cycle. And not sure if this is true for my fellow bleeders, but the full moon is also when my period comes traipsing into town every month.

TMI? OK, back to this thematic dinner ...

The full moon represents the completion of the lunar cycle, making that day a beautiful opportunity to review the previous month and practice gratitude for all that's happened. And since my hormones are also at their peak, I started planning delicious dinners—usually heavy and laden with carbs—to go along with it. Fried chicken with 7-Up Biscuits and mac 'n' cheese. Cavatelli swimming in a ragu that takes all day to simmer down to just the right consistency. Crusty bread seared in a cast iron skillet and then rubbed with so much fresh garlic it makes your toes curl. Full Moon Dinner became a monthly feast and the opportunity for equally delicious conversation.

My kids, a motley crew ranging from age seven to seventeen, are usually accompanied by friends—also of various ages. These teens and preteens tend to be spiritually inclined (or maybe they just like my spaghetti and are willing to feign an interest in deep conversation in order to get it). If friends are available or colleagues from work are around, they're invited. If my boyfriend is in town, he's in, along with his world-famous homemade lasagna. My niece is there whenever she can swing it. Sometimes we bring in a sun-worn table from outside because there are too many people to fit comfortably at the dining table. It's made for six but can technically accommodate ten if you squeeze four people in at the corners and force them to sit in folding chairs from the laundry room. The outside table can get us up to fifteen, and we'll do it because a full moon requires—at least in my opinion—everyone with a seat at the same table. That way, when we get to the question portion of the evening, everyone is included. The Full Moon Dinner is always followed by the *badass question.*

What ***must*** *you let go of in order to be the person you want to be?*

Several months back, I was chatting with author Ben Hardy about his book *Be Your Future Self Now*. We got into a long—and fairly nerdy—discussion about Michelangelo (the artist, not the ninja turtle). Michelangelo's life is a fascinating study in the kind of mindset personal-development geeks obsess over today. He embodied things like flow state, deliberate practice, and the endless opportunities found inside your proximity to power. (I mean, the Medicis? As patrons?! When you were still only a teenager?! OK, bitch, go off!)

And he did all of that *hundreds of years* before anyone would classify what he was doing or have the language to explain why it worked. Of all the things he accomplished (painting, poetry, the Sistine Chapel, etc.), the most incredible, in my humble opinion, is his statue of David. If you ever get the chance to see it in person, you'll be astounded at how massive it is. Unlike the Leaning Tower of Pisa, which will really bum you out by being shockingly smaller than you've been led to believe, the *David* will delight you by being bigger than the giant Philistine he was meant to be fighting.

The attention to detail in the work, the way ancient Carrara marble almost looks like silk or wax because it seems so fluid no matter which angle you look at it from. It's an utter delight to behold—*especially if you happen to be an uncultured American girl on her first trip to Europe.*

It wasn't until nearly two decades after visiting Florence that I sat with Ben Hardy and he told me the coolest thing about how Michelangelo constructed this masterpiece. Apparently Michelangelo said the piece was created *not by carving David out of stone* but by *removing everything that* ***wasn't*** *David.*

Y'all.

Can we all just take a minute?

This iconic work was created not by adding anything ***but by chiseling away at whatever shouldn't be there.***

This is the opposite of everything we're taught.

We're taught to buy more, invest more, add another accolade, procure a new degree, network for one more contact, add another friend, enhance the wardrobe, the house, the job. But what if . . . what if the way we're actually meant to become our best selves is by a careful gleaning? What if we *become* not through addition but through subtraction—through a stripping away of ideas and beliefs and ways of being that we should have never carried in the first place?

My favorite yoga teacher is a wise older man who, deeply on brand, wears tie-dye almost exclusively and travels everywhere with his own harmonium. I happened to take his class on a full moon once, and he mentioned that *that* particular full moon happened to fall under Scorpio. I don't know much about astrology so I can't even tell you what month it was, but I look for signs and lessons in anything. So after class, I googled scorpions.

I never said I was cool, you guys.

In my little research project, I was struck by several things. The first is that in order for a scorpion to grow bigger, it must completely shed its skin first. Its exoskeleton must be hard in order to keep it safe—awesome if you're battling a tarantula but terrible if you'd like to expand in size or strength. If it wants to grow any bigger than it currently is, it must first remove its entire outer layer. Based on an image search, I can tell you that nothing about that process seems easy. In fact, when the scorpion sheds her armor, the shell she leaves behind looks very much like a lifeless version of herself.

I couldn't help but wonder how tight and claustrophobic it must have been constantly pushing against walls that were unable to expand with her. How long did she try to fit inside that smaller version of herself simply because it was easier? How scary it must have been to decide to evolve knowing the transition would be deeply painful. Why am I crying?! And when did I start seeing my story playing out in the life cycle of scorpions? Just wait, it gets even more poignant.

The other beautiful lesson I learned is that when the scorpion finally makes the decision to leave her armor behind, she must live, sometimes for several days, completely vulnerable, without any protective coverings.

My guess is that some of you are in a season like that—a time when you feel raw and exposed and without your armor. It's SO easy in those moments to want to cling to what you know, to crawl back into a skin that no longer fits because at least it comes with certainty. I know this feeling well.

Having gone through harsh, self-appointed transitions many times in my life, I can tell you this: the pain of suffocating in a life too small to accommodate our wholeness is far worse than the discomfort of metamorphosis.

You, my sweet friend, you were not made to be limited by fear. You were made to carve out your own beautiful version of magnificence. Your next evolution will never be found inside a shell that can't support the incredible thing you're becoming.

And so whether this conversation finds you at a new year or on a full moon or any old ordinary day, it's worth your time to ask yourself this question. *What do you need to lay down and leave behind? What* ***must you let go of*** *in order to become a better version of you? What parts and pieces need to be chipped away in order to reveal the masterpiece that is—and always has been—the real and authentic you?*

What ***isn't*** your passion? What's ***definitely not*** your purpose?

Raise your hand if you know exactly what the purpose of your existence is. Throw your other hand up if you have a clearly defined passion that will carry you—fully engaged and excited—all the way through this lifetime without ever once losing momentum?

My guess is that there aren't a whole lot of you holding up the sign for a completed field goal right now.

Figuring out your purpose—literally the reason for your existence—that's the highest level of self-actualization at the very tippy top of Maslow's hierarchy. Not familiar with Abraham Maslow yet? He's one of the founders of humanistic psychology and most famous for something called the *hierarchy of needs*. Imagine the USDA food pyramid, only instead of carbs and vegetables, Maslow organized the foundations of psychological necessity. At the bottom level, the most basic needs are essentials like food, shelter, safety. And at the top? You guessed it: self-actualization.

Meaning we need about a hundred *other* things to fall in line **before** we can ascend to the highest level of consciousness. It's the kind of thing spiritual masters (the Dalai Lama, Morpheus from *The Matrix*, etc.) devote their entire lives to figuring out. So why on earth do you think you're supposed to know your life's purpose at age twenty-seven? Or even fifty-two? Worse yet, why do you think you're somehow failing as a person because you don't?

In a word? Marketing.

Somewhere in the last decade, *knowing your purpose* became popular. Like, Regina George popular. It's right up there with ketogenic diets and staying on top of your Wordle streak.

"Life's Purpose" and her equally sexy sister, "Living with Passion," were invited everywhere. The pursuit of these two ideologies showed up in how-to books and Hallmark movies, Sunday sermons and countless social media posts. If you didn't already know them, you were encouraged to fantasize about them and pursue them relentlessly.

Are you unhappy in life? How about uncertain? Unfulfilled? Unmotivated? Do you have dry skin or male-pattern baldness? Must be because you haven't figured out your purpose! Or perhaps it's because you just need to find your passion. You know, just snap your fingers and discover the one true thing on this earth that will fulfill you above all else.

Oscar Wilde once quipped that *having a grand passion is the privilege of people who have nothing to do*. Said another way, it's pretty freaking hard to pursue something as lofty as life's passion when you're unsure how you're going to make rent this month. But they'll never mention that in those motivational-quote cards your grandma got everyone as stocking stuffers last Christmas. The cards don't really care that you work two jobs while raising three kids or that you're barely keeping your head above water—if you really want to succeed in life, then *you need to know*.

This narrative is sneaky. It feels like guidance. It *seems* helpful—but ultimately, it causes way more harm than good. Not because passion and purpose aren't beautiful pursuits but because what *should be* gorgeous aspirations of an intentional life have become just another thing to collect and show off on Instagram alongside your last trip to Cabo.

It's one more thing you're supposed to have the answer to. Since you likely don't, you can add it to the list of things you already feel shame about—like not eating enough leafy greens and remembering to take calcium supplements to increase bone density.

Look, y'all, **please hear me**: you don't need to know "Your Purpose" to live *with purpose*. And while we're at it, you don't need to have your life's passion figured out to live a beautiful life *you feel passionate about*.

In fact, I don't know a single person who set out to "find their passion" or paid for a course on it or read a book about it who *actually* achieved the desired result.

The most passionate and purpose-filled people I know aren't living for that end goal. They're living for *this* moment, *this* day, *this* creative project, *this* Taco Tuesday with their besties. They're serving that oat milk latte to the customer with a genuine smile on their face. They're taking care of this patient, or client, or student with their core values in alignment and a clear intention about how this moment or circumstance really, truly, is all there is. They're only rarely affected by external circumstances because they understand that their internal world is completely within their control.

I heard an anecdote once about a teacher who invited a Buddhist monk to his class to speak to his students. The monk walked into their classroom without saying a word, then went to the board and wrote something along the lines of "Most of you want to change the world, but you don't want to help Mom do the dishes."

I'm positive I don't have all the pertinent details of that encounter, but I've never forgotten the wisdom of that single sentence. We get these grandiose ideas of how we want to positively affect the world, not realizing that we have the ability to positively affect our immediate surroundings all day, every day.

I was once interviewing candidates for a high-level role at my company. Because it was a big job and because we were so far into the interview process, I did the last round of interviews with each candidate over lunch. One of the women I was considering was ideal: totally polished, utterly professional, and had a résumé filled with accolades. She told me again and again how she'd spent her entire career only working on projects and for companies that positively affect the world. "I care about my impact," she said sincerely. "I believe that what I do matters, and I want to put goodness out there." I was so impressed with her and absolutely loved her intentionality.

Then the server came to take our order . . . and this woman didn't even make eye contact with her. She was short and dismissive. She never said please when ordering or thank you when they brought her drink or her food. In the entirety of the lunch, she barely acknowledged anyone who helped us with our meal but was effusive when she recognized someone she knew at a neighboring table.

Gross.

So despite her résumé and all the lip service about *putting goodness out there*, I knew immediately I didn't want to work with her. But I did think about her—still do.

Imagine the total disconnect of striving for global impact while being a local asshole.

Everyone is so focused on legacy or a statue erected in their honor—they think of "world change" on the largest possible scale. But the majority of people on this planet can't currently make a move that affects "the world." Most of us, if we're really being honest, can only impact the community we come into contact with every day. That's our family, our colleagues at work, our friends, the barista, the crossing guard at your kids' school, the ninety-three people on Instagram who are following us because they like the pictures of our rescue schnauzer.

You might not be able to change "the world," but you can certainly affect *your world* in a positive way. Positive change doesn't mean you need the solution for ridding the oceans of plastic (it's commercial fishing, by the way, not just your Starbucks straw); it means taking the time to do the little meaningful things every day. Smile at a stranger long enough to notice the color of their eyes. Let someone into traffic even though you're in a hurry. Say please and thank you—try to live in such a way that you offer more gratitude than requests. Volunteer your time to help others *without recognition*. Pick up litter wherever you see it—and not just on Earth Day. Remember people's names—you'd be surprised how much it means. If someone is struggling with their stroller, their suitcase, or their homework and you're able, give them a hand. Tell every new mother that she's doing a great job and that you can't believe how good she looks after just having a baby—especially if, like most new moms, she's as vulnerable as a naked mole rat. If you see someone who needs it, give them your seat. Clear the table without being asked. Help with the dishes.

They're all little things—but a handful of little meaningful things everyday adds up to over a thousand meaningful things each year. That's the kind of intention that has ripple effects. It's contagious—it spreads and catches on. Imagine if you influenced one person to do the same, and they influenced another. Your earnest pursuit could shift the vibration of those around you. This can give you more purpose in your day than even the loftiest achievement, and it's far easier to pull off.

Plus, I bet if you look back on your own life, you won't be able to remember all of the people who have achieved really impressive and fancy things. But . . . I guarantee you remember your favorite teacher growing up. I'm positive you know the name of your childhood best friend or a mentor who guided you. I bet you still recall the moment a stranger held the door open as you struggled with your newborn's stroller and as you passed by, they told you, you were doing great.

You can have a lasting impact on someone's life without ever once doing something "the world" deems noteworthy.

Essentially, what I'm proposing here is that it's much easier to live with purpose than it is to know your ultimate purpose. It may just seem like a play on semantics, but the subtle difference between the two matters.

My purpose in life feels very clear and directed . . . at the moment.

I find purpose in being a good mother—though that's a much easier feeling now that my kids are older and I'm not so desperately deep in the weeds.

I find purpose in hosting my podcast—not because I have so much to say; rather, I get to sit with the most interesting people, and I'm grateful for the opportunity to listen.

I find purpose in writing these words for you—though truthfully, I really cannot wait to run out of ideas for nonfiction books so I can start writing exclusively about warrior fairies or something equally geeky.

Purpose in this season of my life looks very different than it did when I was twenty-five or fifteen. Purpose, it turns out, is subject to change. But if I attach **the reason for my existence** to my current focus, it gives far too much weight to what may very well be a passing fancy. It adds far too much pressure to the millions and millions of people who don't feel confident in what they're called to do or who they're supposed to be.

To them I'd like to submit that you don't need to have any idea what your full purpose is right this second to find a lot of purpose *in this moment*. Remember the question from the last chapter? Bring it in here too! You can start not with an attempt to add something to your life but with the intention to take something away. So here we go.

What isn't your purpose?

Are there parts of your life, your work, your relationship that utterly drain you? Are there things you do—even if you're good at them—that you absolutely *hate* but you don't know how to stop? What—or who!—sucks energy out of you like a vampire?

Years ago, while giving a talk about self-care, I asked the audience how they were sleeping. A group of thousands of women (most of whom were mothers) meant that most of them chuckled in response—sleep was not something that many of them felt like they were doing "right."

"Does anyone struggle with insomnia?" Several people near me nodded, and one young woman in particular caught my eye.

"You have insomnia?" I asked her.

She looked a little startled that I'd noticed her—people never expect to be called on until it's too late.

The young woman (I'll call her Paige) stood up and nervously explained that she'd been struggling with insomnia for a year or more. "No matter what I do, I can't seem to fall asleep," she told us. "The longer I stay awake, the more I freak out that I'm still awake, and that makes the anxiety worse."

Around the room many other people nodded in understanding. I asked Paige a lot of questions to try to help her get clarity on what was *really* going on in her life. I won't take you through the full transcript, but allow me to jump ahead to the conclusion.

Paige was in her twenties, and she'd been an ER nurse for a year and a half.

When asked why she went into nursing, she got a little misty eyed and pointed to the woman sitting beside her.

"My mom," she told us. "She's the most amazing person I know, and she's been a nurse my whole life. She's basically a legend at our hospital. I want to be like her."

Beside her, Mama was touched. She got misty eyed too.

"How long have you been doing this work?" I asked her mom.

"Twenty-eight years," she beamed.

"And you love it?"

"I do."

We could all see that she did—you could feel her conviction and, yes, **the purpose** she found in this incredibly vital job she does.

"And how about you, Paige?" I asked. "Do you love being a nurse?"

The young woman who'd been so animated just seconds before about how much she admired her mother froze for a single second. Then she nodded in the affirmative.

"Yes, absolutely."

In my work as an interviewer or a communicator, I have a lot of these kinds of experiences. It's the moment I sense a deeper truth but understand that what's being withheld is for self-preservation purposes *or to guard the feelings of someone else who's listening in.*

In this case, her mother sitting right beside her.

When I'm speaking with someone like this, whether it's an audience member, a reader who comes up at the airport to ask me a question, or even a work colleague seeking advice, I always make sure they truly want my perspective.

Because honestly, sometimes people just want to be heard. They want someone to hold space for them while they process. But—and I can't imagine this will come as a surprise to you—I'm not great at not getting involved. I'm *absolutely terrible* at not giving you advice if there is very clearly advice to be had.

Plus, I don't believe in coincidence. I don't believe I just randomly noticed this girl raising her hand in a sea of thousands. I believe I noticed her because I might be able to help her. Energy works like that—I've never *one time* been giving a speech and called on a nuclear physicist who was looking for clarification on subatomic particles. In that instance, I can't help at all. I'm energetically drawn to people who are wrestling with something I've also battled: in this case, anxiety and insomnia.

"Paige, can I challenge you a little bit?"

She took a deep breath and nodded very seriously.

"Do you *really* love being a nurse?"

She began to turn her head toward her mother.

"No, don't look at Mama. Just look at me."

She did.

"I can tell that your mom is wonderful, and because she's wonderful, I'm positive that she only wants for you to be happy."

Her mother nodded passionately.

"Do you really love being a nurse? Do you even *like* it?"

The room held its breath, and then . . . Paige shook her head no.

The tension came out of her shoulders, and her words came out in a rush. Paige found her job incredibly overwhelming, but she'd pursued it because she wasn't sure what else to do. Her mom was so fulfilled by it, she assumed she'd grow to love it too.

But, dude. *ER nurse??* That's not something you can do lightly.

That's a vocation. That requires a soul-centered commitment and, I'm assuming, a love of adrenaline. And here's this beautiful, gentle daisy trying her best to keep up and assuming she'll "grow into it," all because she's given "too much time to the process to turn back now." AND on top of all that, she wasn't speaking her truth to anyone—especially not her mother—because she was terrified of disappointing her hero.

As a side note, y'all, insomnia is almost always an emotional issue—not a physical one.

By this point, Paige is crying because she was so worried she'd just dropped an irreparable bomb into her relationship with her mother. And Mama is crying because (again, I'm assuming) she just realized her daughter has pursued years and years of hardship in order to please her.

"Well this is *fantastic* news!" I announced. "Because now that you know what you **aren't passionate about**, we can tick that off the list and try another thing that might be right."

It turned out to be horses, by the way.

Horses were what Paige loved—the greatest joy in her life. When she told us all about working with them, her whole essence vibrated with joy. She hadn't pursued that path at all because she worried that she wouldn't be respected for following a path others thought was silly.

I'd like to tell you that today Paige is one of the most successful equine vets west of the Mississippi. I'd like to believe that our conversation all those years ago was the catalyst she needed to pursue life on her terms. I'd like to tell you that, but I honestly don't know what Paige did next.

Maybe she changed everything.

Maybe she kept living out *someone else's purpose* because she wasn't sure what her own was.

The only thing I know for sure is that Paige has a choice, and so do you.

Once she knew for certain what *wasn't* for her, she could use that information to figure out what is. Before you know your purpose or your passion, you sometimes have to try out a lot of things that aren't.

Before you find an incredible romantic partner, you sometimes have to experience pretty terrible people to learn what you don't like.

None of those experiences are failures; they're experiments on the road to clarity. The more experimentation you take part in, the closer you'll get to figuring out your truth.

So why not learn to fly a plane?

Not real airplanes—that's expensive and requires schooling. How about those remote-control airplanes that people meet up in fields to fly together? That always seemed like a cool group of enthusiasts to hang with.

Or you could go to Comic Con dressed as your third-favorite character from your second-favorite Star Wars spin-off. Mine is Chirrut Îmwe. What an absolute badass.

Not into costumes?

Maybe baking? Make your own sourdough starter and study lamination.

Orrrrr you could learn to play the banjo? Join a glee club? Join Sam's Club!

Ooooh! You could try out to be a Dallas Cowboy cheerleader! Then you'd get to meet Kelli and Judy!! How are your jump splits?

Just get out there and try something, try anything at all. Maybe you love it. Maybe you hate it. Maybe you learn to make some bomb croissants.

Either way, it'll be fun.

What **BIG** thing is actually little?

Guys, I wept my way through a Stevie Nicks concert . . . again. It was the *third time* I've seen her perform, and I could *still* barely keep it together. Though, to be fair, I *freaking dare you* to behold Stevie Nicks singing "Landslide" in person and not lose your shit.

When she croons, "I've been 'fraid of changing, 'cause I've built my life around you," don't we all have at least one person in our life who springs to mind?

Your parents?

Your children?

Your younger self?

Taylor Swift?

Somewhere in your existence, you might have experienced the kind of relationship where the edges sort of blur, and you forget where you end and they begin. And *damn it*, then this ethereal being starts serenading with her smoky voice, and all of a sudden, you're a puddle whimpering, *I'm getting older, too . . .*

Because, yeah, you're only forty, but *you feel ancient*, and somehow Stevie Nicks *sees* you.

Ugh! She's too wonderful. I absolutely *adore* her.

I adore her in Fleetwood Mac (my favorite band of all time),

I adore her as a solo artist singing about doves, I even adore her newer collabs with Miley and Lana.

All that adoration is how I found myself crying at a Stevie concert surrounded by twenty thousand other people who were having similar emotional breakthroughs. I danced, I swayed, I vibed, and I sang every word at the top of my lungs . . . just like everyone else around me, except for three people in the seats directly in front of my own.

A woman was seated in between the two men on either side of her, and they were all having a *very* different experience than the rest of us. In a sea of shiny, happy people dancing, they were an island of lame . . . or at least, two of them were.

One was an older teenage boy who looked *miserable*. He was radiating his misery with every neuron he possessed. The other was a man—his dad, I'm assuming—who looked equally bored as he drank one beer after another. Bro may have been there physically, but he was clearly wishing he wasn't. These guys were a hearty stew of negative energy, so thick it could hold a fork upright—the bad vibes simmered off them in waves. The woman sandwiched in between them was about my age, and she took one thousand photos and videos of the concert while she swayed back and forth in her seat.

I felt her.

I felt *for her*, stuck between apathy and ennui, trying to enjoy herself. Her excitement for the experience was palpable, but so was her awareness of the company she kept. She constantly looked from one side to another, nervously checking, gauging, *hoping* . . .

Have you ever been really excited about something but you're with people who don't get it—or worse, downright hate it?

I know that particular energy so well.

I used to constantly invite people to experiences (concerts, art shows, spin classes, various continents) that the invitee wasn't really interested in.

I invited them because (a) I was super into whatever the event was, and since I am down to try just about anything once, I figure other people like being invited to new things as much as I do, or (b) (and this one is far more relevant for today's chat) because I really wanted to go and it literally never occurred to me that I could go to something alone.

I am, by nature, an explorer.

I love and cherish the comfort of my home, but I have a perpetual case of wanderlust. I will choose experiences over things one hundred times out of ten.

That awareness wasn't fully formed for me yet as a young adult. How could it be? I'd barely lived at all when I got into my first relationship when I was only nineteen, and since he was so much older and since I grew up in a culture that was like, "You should get married immediately, and also your husband knows best because he has a penis, blah blah blah," it never occurred to me to feed my passion for adventure. He was the head of our household and a homebody, so that meant that "we" were homebodies.

For years and years, we did the same things, ate the same foods, went to the exact same restaurant on the same day every week—and no shade to all my enneagram type 5s who live for that sort of ritual and routine; I love that for you. But when you're young, and you haven't yet built your sense of self (and don't even know that you're allowed to have one), and a voice of authority says, *This is who* ***we*** *are*, you're like, *OK, groovy*! You have no idea how to find your own identity yet, so you just adopt theirs.

It reminds me of that old expression about judging a fish by its ability to climb a tree. When we force ourselves to fit into spaces that are incongruent with our true selves, it will always feel wrong.

In fact, the only person who *will* be comfortable is the person asking us to change shape to fit into their box with them.

Imagine someone you love buys you a beautiful pair of *very expensive*, very tall high-heel stilettos—**that are two sizes too small for your feet**. You can tell she's really proud of this thing she's giving you . . . after all, Louboutin is *her favorite brand*, and this is the exact size *she* wears. You can appreciate the lovely gesture—this friend always looks so fabulous in her shoes, and she cared enough to get you some. Plus, you don't really know what kind of shoes would suit you anyway, so you go for it. You squeeze yourself into someone else's ideal and learn to make it work. She's happy because she's been able to influence you to be more like her—validating her choices. But you're the one who gets blisters.

Only you don't realize that at first. You're grateful to have someone else's guidance, and you assume . . . this is just the way "we" do things.

I would get these wild pangs to go do something—*anything*—that was different from the same routine over and over again. I'd sign up for a half marathon and talk someone from work into doing it too. I'd see an ad for an interesting play and beg my husband to join me. Pasadena's annual "show house" would open for viewing, and I'd convince my dad to drive four hours to walk through with me. *That one was worth it though; if there's one thing Pasadena does well, it's classic architecture and Waspy interior designers with impeccable taste.*

Sometimes I could get a buddy to come along on my schemes, and if they ended up digging the experience, it was the absolute *best*.

But more often than not, when you invite someone to something you're super into but they're only lukewarm about—especially if you're a people pleaser—it typically just ruins the whole experience for **you**, the person who actually, really wanted to be there.

Look, despite what the internet would have us believe, most people aren't narcissists. If they get to your musical or your Renaissance fair or your meeting for organic gardeners to discuss the importance of urban plants in a city's overall ecosystem (a real thing I signed up to attend once), most people will politely endure it for you even if they're bored.

The problem is that if you're a people pleaser (a.k.a. you likely have childhood trauma that forced you to be hypersensitive to the emotions of others in order to survive), you are incapable of ***not knowing*** that they're bored. And so you feel terrible because you invited them to this thing, and you're actually quite enjoying yourself, which somehow makes the fact that they *aren't* enjoying it so much worse. So you'll get overly chirpy and bright eyed like a cheerleader trying to hype them into loving this chamber orchestra as much as you do.

Or you'll feel super anxious.

Or maybe angry.

Or perhaps bitter.

To circumnavigate the way you're feeling, you'll suggest that you're really *not that into this either, so why don't you just leave and go do something they want to do instead?* OR you'll make like sister-friend at the Stevie Nicks concert and enjoy one of your favorite singers of all time in what is likely one of her last tours, and you'll do it while absorbing the negative energy of the two men on either side of you.

And those two bros surrounding her? They weren't even *trying to pretend* they were happy to be there—or at the very least, happy for *her* to be there.

Now maybe you're thinking, *Rach, it sounds like you're projecting. You can't possibly know that woman and how she felt about Stevie. And you definitely don't know each member of that family and their individual motivations for the energy they were putting into the world.*

Fair. But I stand by my assessment based on one single thing: **That woman was desperate to get up and dance.**

She was swaying in her seat and looking around at all the other women (myself included) who were vibing out. Basically, the only thing missing from this becoming a full-on coven gathering was a bubbling cauldron! She very nearly levitated through "Gold Dust Woman," whose beat is basically daring its listener not to sway along.

She never did stand up to dance because as often as she watched others around her, she also obsessively glanced at the men on either side of her. She was constantly trying to gauge just how annoyed both of them were to be there.

I've been in that exact scenario too many times to count. Maybe you have too.

Here's the thing though: it's not those two douche lords' fault. It's not your mama's fault or your girlfriend's fault or your husband's fault that you/we find ourselves in these situations. It's our fault. We own it completely.

A couple of years ago, my niece told me she was bummed because she couldn't take the road trip she'd been dreaming about. I was so confused about this pronouncement because she worked for me at the time, and my company has unlimited paid vacation days. When I asked her why she couldn't go, she explained that she couldn't find anyone *to go with her*. She was twenty-eight years old at the time.

Guys, when you're an adult, you can 100 percent go on a road trip by yourself. In fact, it's one of my favorite ways to travel. You can listen to audiobooks or your favorite podcast. You can put on a groovy playlist to daydream or, if it's been a minute since you've had a good cry, put on the *Beaches* soundtrack and get super deep in your feelings.

You can go to dinner by yourself and on vacation by yourself too. You can go sit in the lobby bar of the best hotel in your town and **pretend** to be on vacation . . . *by yourself.* Make up an alias and a tortured backstory. Wear a caftan or maybe a tuxedo. You can do anything at all that sounds fun and *you can do it totally alone.*

It's really, truly not that big of a deal.

For some people I know, the idea of sitting alone at a restaurant is akin to being eaten alive by fire ants. In fact, I bet some of you read my paragraph above about a solo road trip and thought, *A young woman can't travel alone! She'll be murdered or trafficked or conned into joining a sex cult!*

And truthfully, that's exactly the kind of response I got from my niece.

"Who says?" I asked her.

"My mom? Auntie? Grammy? The women in our family aren't really the kind who travel alone."

This is when I pointed out that I am a woman in our family, and I often travel alone. I've done it for decades. I have yet to join a sex cult.

Why do we constantly heed the advice of people *who have* ***never done*** *the thing we're interested in doing*?!

Most of the time the fear we have about something—the "big" stuff in life that terrifies us—it's not even our own fear. That fear comes from our family or friends. The fear comes from the unknown: we've never seen it done before, so we're not even sure it's allowed. Sometimes our fears are legitimate; other times they're ridiculous. The reality is our lives will have plenty of justifiable reasons to be afraid . . . enjoying an activity by yourself isn't one of them. Going somewhere alone is minuscule on the list of mole hills disguising themselves as mountains in our imagination.

Look at your own life: identify something that you're making way too big of a deal about and then just . . . go do the thing you've been avoiding. Discover that you will live through it. Repeat.

Need to have a difficult conversation with someone? Yes, it sucks and it's hard, but stop being a pansy and just push through it. You'll feel one thousand times better, and you'll have a thicker skin the next time you need to talk about something hard.

Are you struggling emotionally and you're pretty sure that therapy will help, but the idea of starting it up feels so daunting? Yeah, I know how you feel. Most of us are rolling around with—at best—the emotional equivalent of Pandora's box in our chest. At worst, you open up and allow some of those emotions to surface, and it's like the scene in *Indiana Jones* where they open the Ark of the Covenant and everyone's face melts off.

Working through your stuff is really hard, but the rewards for you—and literally everyone you interact with—*are so, so worth it.*

Stop putting it off. Make the call, finish the project, ask for the promotion, say how you feel, go see your favorite band all by yourself.

In yoga class, they always say the hardest part of a yoga practice is just getting to your mat. It's the same with anything in your life that seems big or scary or daunting. When you just finally face it, you'll discover that it's actually really just not that big a deal. But you are. You are, in fact, the only truly big and powerful thing in this equation.

What little thing is actually **BIG**?

If we're going to talk about things that just *aren't* that big of a deal, we should probably also look at the reverse. Is it possible there's something in your life you don't give a ton of weight to that actually has massive implications?

This is a rhetorical question, guys. The answer is obviously yes.

Little things that are actually a big deal can be awesome. Like thinking he was just a buddy, then realizing he's the love of your life. They can also be negative, like finally understanding that some "little" thing from your childhood actually messed you up way more than you realized. When I think of all the counseling sessions I did over the years to process those "little" things from my childhood. Ha! I hope my therapist bought a boat with the proceeds.

Or perhaps the little thing you're ignoring is how you allow yourself to be treated. Maybe there's a real monster in your life. Maybe it's hiding *in* your bed instead of under it. Maybe you're not giving enough attention to that "silly little hobby" of yours, wrongly assuming your passion project will never amount to anything. Maybe you give up on your health journey again and again because you're not seeing results as quickly as you'd like. Who cares if you keep going, right? It's just a little thing.

Don't forget that the Grand Canyon was carved into the earth one drop of water at a time. The little things in our life can have profound effects.

Little things can be big things. Situations we thought were monumental might end up as nothing much at all. The only way to know the difference is to know yourself.

Personal autonomy is your birthright. As babies, we come into this world telling anyone within earshot that we're hungry or cold or unhappy. We express ourselves completely with our whole tiny bodies.

Even as we get a bit older, we still fight for our space, our toys, the same number of marshmallows as our big brother has in his mug. If my eleven-year-old and my seven-year-old sit beside each other in *any* capacity, they will be fighting over their personal space in under ninety seconds flat. This is why they invented minivans—you thought it was for the sliding rear doors, but really it's to keep these punks away from each other lest someone puts one finger into someone else's airspace and World War III begins.

We had it when we were kids, but somewhere between birth and adulthood, most of us lose the ability to speak up for ourselves.

We learn to please.

We learn to appease.

We learn to show up in the way that we believe will garner us the most love.

In doing so, we lose piece after piece of our true selves. This is terrible for about a thousand reasons, but I'd like to circle around a central thesis today, which is: if you lose touch with your ability to speak up over little things that bother you, you will either (a) begin to gaslight yourself into believing that they don't actually bother you or (b) know that they bother you but feel unable to express it because you value someone else's opinion over your own.

Both options suck.

Both options, if continued in perpetuity, will cut your connection with self and remove your access to your personal intuition. The list of people who have told me they "don't have intuition" is endless. But if we dig a little deeper (and spend a couple hours hoovering a cheese board while we talk), those same people will admit to spending the last several *decades* ignoring or denying their own feelings.

Imagine that you have a fantastic and beautiful friend who loves you unconditionally and who always has the exact right answer to anything you're wondering. Your friend is basically a magical fairy (the ethereal ones from *Lord of the Rings*, not the pirate kind from the last *Tinker Bell* spin-off). Now imagine that every single time this amazing friend tries to say anything to you, you ignore her. Doesn't matter what it is—a piece of advice, a warning, a compliment—whenever your friend says anything, you argue with her about why she's wrong or simply pretend she didn't say anything at all.

How long would it take before your friend stopped trying?

How long would it be before her voice got smaller and smaller until it was barely audible?

This is exactly what happens with our intuition.

That still, small voice inside you has tried and tried to tell you you're beautiful and worthy, but you argue that you're not. It *yells* that this person is no good, that there's something inherently wrong with your pairing. You ignore it. When you later discover exactly how toxic they were, you cry and lament, *How could I not have seen this before?* That perfect, magical friend shrinks even smaller inside of you.

The problem is not that you don't have intuition; the problem is that you've built up bigger and bigger walls to block out your own voice until you can't hear yourself anymore. Pretty wild that you have impenetrable boundaries in place against yourself and very few against anybody else. It's almost as if your own true self can't exist simultaneously with people or situations who don't respect it, and so you must silence whichever of the two you value the least.

In other words, you won't be able to tell whether something *is* just a little annoyance or truly *not that big a deal* because at this point, you can't trust your own perspective. The only way you can trust your own perspective is if you are in a loving and healthy relationship **with yourself**.

Are you familiar with bonsai trees?

It's a non sequitur, I know, but stick with me.

You know those really cool miniature trees made popular by Japanese artists? They've been trendy since the 1800s because each one looks like a fully grown, big-ass tree but in teeny format. Do you know *why* they all look like fully grown, big-ass trees? Because bonsai trees actually ***are*** big-ass trees!

A bonsai tree, if left to its own devices, would grow to be big and bold just like any other tree in nature. So why don't you know that?

Because at some point in history, an arborist discovered that if you kept the bonsai in a tiny container, it wouldn't realize it was meant to be big—it would grow only to the edges of its pot.

It would only grow as big as the box someone else put it in.

**tap tap* Is this thing on?*

The little thing that's actually big? **It's you.**

You are the magical fairy creature with the best advice and intuition.

You are the one who knows what's good and true and right for you.

You are the being capable of manifesting anything you can imagine.

You are powerful beyond measure.

You are big—so why do you keep playing so small?

Why do you keep letting people treat you as less than you're worth?

If you're not sure, don't worry, I have a theory.

I don't think it's possible for any of us to have a healthy relationship with the world around us if we don't have a healthy relationship with ourselves.

One of the scriptures I was taught to memorize as a child said, "Greater is He who is in me than he who is in the world." As a girl, I always loved the idea that God is in each of us. As an adult, I was happy to discover that many other religious practices have a similar view.

That "still, small voice" <u>is</u> us.

It's also the divine creator / source / God or whatever you want to call Her. Your intuition is divinely given, and when you separate yourself from it, you separate yourself from the source.

No wonder you feel lost. No wonder it's easy to feel small—you've forgotten that you're a part of something cosmic and divine. Rumi said it best: "You are not a drop in the ocean; you are the entire ocean in a drop."

You are the whole damn thing.

You. Not the person *they* would prefer. Not the good girl who knows exactly what to say to please others. Not the golden boy who follows precisely the right path that will make Mama and Daddy most proud. YOU. You *as you are* . . . or maybe it's more accurate to say "You *as you were*" before they told you who to be to please them best.

Don't speak so loudly.
Don't be so bossy.
Stop being so sensitive.
Why can't you be more like your sister?

They're just little digs. But they stack on top of one another—they tell us exactly who to be by telling us exactly what not to do. Enough time goes by (it doesn't take long) and you don't even realize that you have no idea who you actually are because you lost yourself somewhere along the way.

Remember when you used to want to be an astronaut? A painter? A coach?

Remember when you loved death metal? Or when you were on the team? When you played that sport that always made you feel alive? Remember when you had the time of your life? Remember what excitement feels like? When was the last time you felt it sizzle through your veins and ignite the fireworks in your brain? When was the last time you couldn't fall asleep not because you were anxious or unsure but because you were too busy dreaming?

You are the little thing that's actually big.

You are a bonsai tree. You only need to step outside the box they put you in, and your branches will naturally begin to stretch upward to the sun.

When did you know something was wrong?

I'm what they call an "Oprah baby."

An admittedly niche term for latchkey kids like me who came home from school every day and watched *The Oprah Winfrey Show*. Basically, Oprah was our babysitter and, on some deeper level, the mythical mother figure we all dreamed of having.

I have seen every single episode—and once they released the show on DVD to celebrate twenty-five seasons, I rewatched the classics yet again.

I genuinely worry for younger generations who might know Oprah as an icon but have no idea why she's so important. Y'all are never going to experience the magic of enjoying a midafternoon snack on the carpet in front of a TV with only six channels. On one of those local affiliates, Oprah taught us about redesigning your home, or how to access your higher self, or what shape your poo should be if you're eating right.

(It's an *S*, by the way.)

We learned how to cook pasta and discovered what to buy for Christmas and never ceased to be charmed by how only one of Julia Roberts's eyes would water when she was a guest. Even the Pretty Woman feels nervous around Oprah.

Since I've seen every episode, many of their lessons live in my brain in perpetuity. They're forever part of the childhood knowledge you never forget—like the phone number you had when you were eight: 845-5465.

One episode that has always stuck out for me more than most—probably because I was *way* too young to be watching it—was the conversation Oprah had with Gavin de Becker about his book *The Gift of Fear*. The conversation that day (based on the book I would read years later) was about the signals we receive from our body that warn us of danger. What I learned was that intuitively, our bodies *always* know when something isn't right—even if our mind is too disconnected to listen.

The idea I've never forgotten and that I still reference regularly twenty-four years later is *humans are the only animal that will sense danger and keep walking toward it.*

Think about it, a deer or a dog or a ring-tailed lemur—if they have a sense that something is wrong? They're out. They don't debate it or rationalize or consult with their friends first. They *trust their intuition* and go.

Humans on the other hand have been taught again and again to ignore the voice inside of us that tells us something isn't right. This is wildly dangerous when the situation actually *is* life threatening. But on a more basic level, ignoring what your body is telling you leads to the majority (if not all) of the most painful experiences of our life.

The devastating breakup you went through after realizing your girlfriend was a covert narcissist. The business partner who ended up taking all the credit and most of the profit before leaving you to clean up the mess from all the bridges they burned. The new job that seemed so great at the beginning but ended up being a soul-sucking nightmare.

I'm not talking about the regular real-life tensions and

annoyances that will affect every human. I'm talking about the experiences where you feel bamboozled, like your life just went ass over elbow and you've gotten way far off course. You look up one day in bewilderment and think, *How did everything go so wrong?*

If I asked you to, I'm sure you could come up with times in your own life when you were left wondering, *What just happened?*

What *just happened* is that you ignored the intuitive, animal instinct that tried to protect you.

You know how I know that people keep ignoring it? Because I can always trace my personal blunders back to the moment when *I should have known*—and done better. And so I've learned to ask myself and others, ***When did you know something was wrong?***

Not "When did it ***go*** wrong?" but *When did you know something was wrong?*

Because here's the thing: we *always* sense something isn't right long before it ever goes wrong. Every single time I sit with a friend or my kids *or myself*, and we're working through the emotional saga they're living through, this question will always stop the story right in its tracks. After I ask it, there's usually a moment of wonder or shock, anger or embarrassment as they realize the truth. Often, they sensed the truth months (or years) before. Sometimes it was in the very first moment they met the person that would become such a destructive force in their life.

"She was always so sweet when we hung out alone," a friend of mine told me over coffee recently. "But then when we went out in a group, she was so different. She became kind of jealous and rude—even her face changed. It was like, I don't know, harder. None of my friends liked her, and they like everyone."

Just like Bieber's mama.

This particular girl ended up being a nine-month saga of chaos and drama for my pal.

"And when did you know something was wrong?" I asked him.

This normally confident man looked a bit sheepish. "Honestly? On our second date. Yeah, she was so sweet, but there was this moment . . . she said something rude about a stranger at the bar, and it made me feel weird."

"Weird how?"

"Like, kind of sick to my stomach. But I told myself she was just kidding around, and I brushed it off."

"And now?"

"Now I realize *that moment*, that was who she is. God! If I would have just ended things then . . ."

At another dinner, an author friend and I worked together to finish a bottle of Sancerre while rehashing a big project. Her work had become successful, and over the last few years, she'd watched her books turned into a movie. From the outside looking in, the process had seemed like a fairy tale, something most authors dream about. From the inside, though, it had been an utter nightmare. The producer she sold her book rights to ended up being awful; they alienated one actor after another and made the set hostile and toxic. Though in the pitch meetings they'd promised to stay true to the beloved characters and the storyline, almost immediately, those things were changed in order to be sexier or more commercial. She is rightfully, deeply protective of her work and the fans who made the books a success, but once the project was in motion, it was a runaway train that couldn't be stopped. In the end, this friend would rather have forgone the Hollywood experience and the money and the red carpets to have not lost multiple years and creative control of the characters she'd spent a decade creating.

We were sitting in a little bistro in Brooklyn when she told me all about it.

"But when did you know something was wrong?" I prompted her.

The tension came out of her shoulders as she exhaled.

"Damn, Rachel, I knew in the first meeting with that producer! He had the résumé and the clout, and he said all the right things, but something just felt off."

"So why did you go through with it?"

She laughed at herself and shook her head.

"Because it all seemed so glamorous. Having a movie made? Imagine it. And everybody is so impressed and buzzy, and they're all telling you what a big deal it is. Who on earth would say no?"

And that's the thing, most of us don't say no. Most of us don't even say, "Can we slow down for a moment so I can think this through?" We allow people to rush us and push us into action we're not ready for.

I'm not talking about bad or hard situations we knowingly take on because we have no choice. Needs must. Sometimes you say yes to the gig, the apartment, your dad's new girlfriend because that's what has to be done. Life isn't always easy or fair; occasionally you gotta do what you gotta do.

But there are plenty of times when a choice—at this exact moment—isn't necessary. We're so tantalized by the possibilities we imagine in our head—the perfect job, partner, vacation, experience—that we inadvertently slot something/anything into that role, regardless of whether or not the puzzle pieces actually fit together.

"When you don't know what to do, do nothing." That's an Oprah quote too, guys. She has wisdom for every situation.

Unfortunately, most don't slow down long enough to do a gut check. We care so much about whether something *looks* right, we don't stop to ask if it *feels* right. Or worse than that, we don't say *no* or *stop* or *I'm unsure* because we don't want to be rude or we fear we'll miss out on our big chance.

You know that Eminem song "Lose Yourself"?

Of course you do—it's a classic!

It came on the radio the other day, and I was singing every word like I was about to challenge Papa Doc in a rap battle. But for the first time ever, the words hit me differently: *Do not miss your chance to blow / This opportunity comes once in a lifetime, yo.*

I mean, yes, but also no, not at all.

This particular day, this moment, and any opportunity that comes along with it? Yes, that's a *once-in-a-lifetime* thing because everything is. Every single moment, every breath, every third Saturday—it's all once in a lifetime. I hope holding that awareness will make it all feel more sacred and precious and allow you to be present in it.

But.

There's no such thing as your *one shot.*

It's only "one shot" if you miss it and then quit.

Otherwise, it's just an experience added to the list of things you experimented with on the way to inventing who you become.

After a decade working at it, I finally got to the place in my career where I get to work and travel as a keynote speaker. I'm most often tapped to hype up a crowd, especially if that crowd is filled with a lot of X chromosomes. I am confident enough to tell you, after a lot of years being terrible at it, I'm pretty good now. And *the most tepid response* I've ever received from an audience was when I was the opening keynote for Oprah *freaking* Winfrey.

Dude, we've already established what she means to me, and my biggest onstage *wah-wah* happened in front of her! Can you imagine how tragic that must have felt to an Oprah baby?

I felt like I'd waited my whole life for that moment; I'd imagined it for years. I wrote the idea of it down in my journal hundreds and hundreds of times, visualizing it again and again long before I had the clout or the ability to make it come true. *This is your shot*, my friends told me. *If you nail this, maybe you get your own show, or maybe she becomes your mentor! OMG, maybe she invites you to Montecito for a sleepover!!* The list of possibilities we came up with in the car ride to Barclays Center in Brooklyn was endless. I went into that speech feeling so grateful and excited about *what dreams may come.*

I went onstage and gave a talk the way I usually do—it was filled with lots of energy, at least one Justin Timberlake dance break, and a story about how I once lost a tampon in my body for two weeks. Humor is always the foundation of my work—and I wanted to be that way that day—even in front of Oprah.

On every other occasion I've told that story onstage, the audience laughs so hard, they can't catch their breath. So I've shared it a lot, intentionally telling a story to embarrass myself. I do it because I assume everyone in the crowd is a bit like me—maybe they also look at the speakers in their structured jumpsuits and flawless makeup and the imbued authority the stage offers and maybe it makes them believe that the person talking is somehow more special than they are. But if I can stand onstage and tell you a story that's funny and, yes, kind of gross, I hope it makes you realize that we're all a little gross sometimes, and nobody on that stage is more special than you are, no matter how good her blazer looks.

And you know what? That was just not the crowd for it.

Fourteen thousand people were there for the wisdom and the upper echelon of classy that is Oprah and Michelle Obama, and here comes your girl Rach, wearing Levi's and talking about the way the tampon looked when it finally fell out of my body—like a recently hatched chicken—and it just didn't, well, *land* very well.

Were there people in the audience laughing? Yep.

Was Oprah one of them? Absolutely not.

In fact, at the end of my speech, Oprah came onstage for a previously planned Q+A, and as she walked up, I tried to tell myself that I hadn't bombed in front of her the way I thought I did.

"Giiiirl," she said in front of that gigantic crowd, "I'm glad you got to the point because I had no idea where you were going with that tampon story."

I absolutely died. My body was upright, but to this day, I have no idea how I managed to keep a smile on my face. Fifteen minutes of Q+A were still left with my idol, and all I could think about was that I'd totally failed in front of her. Worse still? I had failed by being *myself.*

My dreams of slumber parties in Montecito went up in smoke.

But then a small miracle happened. I don't know where it came from because I was close to throwing up, but the universe offered hope, and I found a little courage. I came out of my daze, and there she was, telling me how she'd noticed my work and had watched my book's success. Then she leaned toward me and asked me why I thought people like my writing.

I took a deep breath and explained that as a woman, I feel like there are a whole host of real-life things we go through, but we're not supposed to talk about them because they're not polite to say out loud—so then we all just suffer and struggle silently thinking something is wrong with us.

"I think maybe people like that I tell stories about things like tampons getting stuck inside my body. It's real."

Some women in the audience applauded and cheered—I knew there were at least a few people like me out there! Oprah nodded in what I took to be understanding, which was enough for me.

I never heard from her team again.

Did that bum me out? Absolutely.

Did it stop my career or keep me from communicating in my own style?

Y'all, if it did, I wouldn't be here writing these words now.

There's no such thing as a single shot at love or success or life, and if you buy into that myth, it will push you into situations that your gut—the seat of your inner wisdom—is trying to warn you against.

So. When did *you know* something was wrong?

Try a meditation or a journaling session and take a look at the negative experiences you've had in the last five years. Slow down long enough to ask yourself, Was there a moment of pause? Was there a feeling? Was there ever a sense that I was walking down the wrong path?

Chances are that you'll find one.

When you do, pay attention to exactly what you felt—What did your body do? Did your heart speed up? Did your stomach feel sick? Did you just *know* that something was off but you didn't know what? If you can begin to identify some of the sensations you had in the past, it will help you to identify them when they show up in the future.

What are you attracting?

Once upon a time my company and the team that supported it were much larger. We had the most darling office in West Austin filled with such incredible personalities and energy that just walking through the door in the morning made me happy. At the time, the team was constantly expanding; it seemed every time I would leave on a business trip, I would come back to discover a new person who had joined our motley crew in my absence. With so much growth, it was important to have a touchstone to hold on to at least one thing that would remain the same despite the change that was constantly present in a start-up culture. That one thing was our team meeting.

Once a week we'd gather for a team meeting that always began with a gratitude share and then inevitably moved to the goals we were working toward as a group. When we began to work from home during the pandemic, we kept this tradition alive by moving our team meeting to one giant Zoom call, which made it fun to see everyone's home decor style or, in the case of some of the single guys on our production team, a shocking lack thereof.

It was on one of those Zoom calls where we found ourselves discussing goal setting, a theme in the content we were creating that week. I asked members of the group to share if they had any personal goals they were working on. Tish, a young woman on the marketing team, offered her intention.

"Well, I'd really like to manifest more. I want to get into that. I don't manifest at all right now, and I'd like to make that something I try."

Now, as her mentor, I absolutely loved this vision she had. But as the person who had been teaching on ideas surrounding the law of attraction and manifesting on the podcast, in keynotes, and in my writing—all of which she'd consumed—I realized I had missed a key element as a teacher. Tish—and therefore probably loads of other people I'd talked about this concept to—didn't understand a crucial element.

You can't "start manifesting" or "stop manifesting," you simply *are manifesting*. You are constantly attracting things to your life—both good and bad—whether you want to or not.

Now let's back up and allow me to explain, in case manifesting is not something you're already familiar with. Back in the early 2000s, a woman named Rhonda Byrne came out with a book called *The Secret*. I was thirteen at the time, so my only knowledge of the book or its contents was inside an episode of *The Oprah Winfrey Show* (obviously). I'm fairly certain I wasn't allowed to watch that episode because whatever "the secret" was, it *wasn't* the Bible, and so my parents didn't trust it.

It wasn't until decades later that I happened to see *The Secret* movie, which was on YouTube (and I think still is), where you could watch it for free. The production quality of the movie notwithstanding, there are perspectives and ideas in it I'd never heard before—the most notable of which was the concept of the law of attraction. Full disclosure, I actually don't love a lot of the angles the experts in that documentary use, since many of them focus almost exclusively on wealth, which just ends up feeling a bit creepy. But. Their explanation of manifesting and attraction and raising your vibration is right on. That documentary, with its cheesy cutaways to the Knights Templar over a dramatic orchestral soundtrack, is a fantastic jumping-off point if you've never heard about the topic before. And I will forgive the cheese and even the hard sell on becoming a millionaire because it was a documentary film from 2006, and, well, it could have been much worse.

What that particular movie did for me was give me language for something I'd never known how to explain. If you looked at the full story of my family of origin, the place I grew up, the environment I was raised in, and the constant trauma of the first sixteen years of my life . . . none of what came after it makes *any* sense at all.

Nothing in my formative years seemed to point toward the life I live today. Not the career success or the financial, not the healthy relationship with myself, my partner, or my children—I had no example of any of these things. But if you had asked me to explain it or pick one single thing that contributed to my success the most, it's my imagination.

Seriously.

For as far back as I have memory, I have been a daydreamer. I'm guessing this is something I developed very early on as a coping mechanism, a means of escaping reality and taking myself somewhere else. As a very young girl, the escape was inside of fairy tales or the books I read. But when I became a teenager and started to learn more about the world, the place I took myself to in my mind was a real one.

Los Angeles.

I grew up two hours north and a world away from Los Angeles, but as soon as I knew it existed, I thought about it obsessively. From the time I was twelve until I left home at seventeen, it was a single thought in my mind every single day of my life. I imagined where I would live and what I would do for a job to afford my cool Hollywood apartment. I imagined life soon and life ten years from now. I pored over magazines and devoured TV shows (the internet didn't really exist properly yet, kids). I surrounded myself with cutouts taped to the wall. I wrote about LA in the pages of my journal and talked about it constantly with my friends. Every time life got especially hard—which was often enough—I would take myself out of the situation into my imagination. I ended up graduating from high school a year early, and since both my parents had stopped being interested in parenting long before that, nobody fought me when I said that I was saving up my money to move to LA. Before I was eighteen years old, I had an apartment in Hollywood, multiple crappy jobs to help support myself, and an internship at Miramax Films (one of the absolute hardest gigs to land) despite the fact that I was underage and didn't have a college degree.

While none of the years that followed were a breeze, in hindsight, there were moments in time where I really was in the exact right place at the exact right time, and I had enough meager skill to raise my hand for the chance to try.

Every single opportunity, failure or success, felt so independent from one another at the time—but looking back, I can see how they all stacked on top of one another to get me to where I am today. And it all started with that big move to LA. A big move to LA precipitated by a full decade of daydreaming about doing just that. What I didn't understand at the time is that what I would call daydreaming and imagination was actually laser-focused intention that would help me figure out how to make my dreams a reality.

I manifested that destiny because I simply refused to see anything but that. Every road I traveled, every door I walked through was only ever leading one place because I only seemed to notice the little opportunities that led to my desired destination. That is, at its most basic level, the concept of the law of attraction. It's the idea that anyone can attract something into their life by focusing on it with intention, but this really only tells a small part of a much bigger story. The law of attraction says you can attract what you want, but as Dr. Wayne Dyer once explained so perfectly, *You don't manifest what you want; you manifest what you are.*

Energetically, each and every one of us functions at different levels of vibrational output. This part isn't *woo-woo* hippie stuff (I'll get to that in a minute); this is quantum physics. We're all putting out different levels of vibrational energy, and I don't care how much you buy into this or not, you have to admit that you've experienced this yourself.

If you walk into an elevator, and the person inside it is joyful and happy and having a fantastic day, it *feels very different* than getting into the elevator with someone who is pissed off and seething. In fact, the person in the elevator doesn't have to say anything to you—you can sense that the joyful person is joyful, and you can feel when you've just encountered someone who's ready to explode.

Have you ever stopped to ask yourself *why* you can sense that? It's because we radiate our emotions. In both examples I gave, the emotions are at extreme ends of the spectrum, so they're easy for almost anyone to pick up on, but even the duller emotions like apathy or boredom have their own energetic signatures.

Now again with the science, every single thing in this world, solar system, universe is made up of energy. Period. When you break things down to their most basic elements, it's all energy. We are made up of atoms, atoms are made up of protons and neutrons, and at the center of it all is pure energy. Energy is the core of everything, which is why you'll hear so many wise teachers and gurus say that we are all connected and all the same.

The only difference between me and an oak tree is the way

the energy orients itself—and also, one of us has far more junk in their trunk.

If we are energy, and our thoughts and emotions can be detected and measured as energy as they leave our body, it explains why like attracts like.

Have you ever been having a great morning, and it seems to get better as the day goes on? Something nice happens, a kind driver lets you into traffic during rush hour, and while it's simple courtesy, it brightens your day because that on-ramp is usually really stressful. *What luck!* The easy on-ramp means you've got a little extra time to stop for coffee, and while you order, you chat happily with the barista. She seems to be in a great mood too, and when she compliments your favorite earrings, it perks you up even more. Now you're chuffed up and feeling really great when you realize that they did an absolutely *perfect* job on the ratios of your oat milk cappuccino—which rarely happens. *What a time to be alive!* The remaining drive to work is a breeze because your favorite song from high school comes on in the last ten minutes, and even though as a feminist you know you shouldn't be enjoying the words to the Ying Yang Twins quite this much, you crank the music in the car and scream every word.

Y'all skeet skeet skeet skeet.

The reverse is also true. We've all had a day that goes from bad to worse—the fact that "from bad to worse" is an expression just proves it!

Now back to my young colleague and her desire to "manifest more." The goal can't be to manifest more because you already are doing that simply by existing. The goal then is to manifest and attract things to us with *intention*.

I have a family member who is always sick. Always. If it's not a cold, it's the flu. If it's not the flu, her allergies are "acting up" or she's having an extreme reaction to her lactose intolerance or the person at the next table has on cologne that's too strong and it's making her nauseous. There's always something ailing her. When she's not sick, she spends all her time worrying about when she will get sick again.

The energy/vibration/focus of her mind, body, and spirit has been set to "illness" for decades. She has long since decided that she's cursed with a bad immune system and destined for a life of disease. I genuinely worry that each medical anomaly will continue to grow in severity until she attracts something that will kill her. There is nothing more powerful than the thoughts we think and the energy we attach to them. All she focuses on is sickness, and since our minds tell our body what is real, I'm positive she is actively weakening her immune system. Couple that with the fact that the message she sends to the universe is *I don't want to get sick, I don't want to get sick, I don't want to get sick.* The universe, however, is only responding to her vibrational energy and her focus. The universe doesn't "hear" *I don't want to*, it **feels** the vibration of her fear and worry (very low-level vibrations to attract), and it gets the focus of her attention: *Sick. Sick. Sick.*

Now we're into the woo-woo hippie stuff.

The same is true for our romantic partners, our jobs, and our circles of friends. In life, there are freak moments, accidents occur, shit happens . . . but our consistent themes—the scenarios that play out again and again—those are never flukes, or luck, or destiny. Those are something you've got to take responsibility for.

The fact that you keep dating men who are emotionally unavailable, and no matter how great they seem at the beginning, they end up running off with your cousin or stealing your car? One of those is a fluke. Three times and it's a pattern, of which *you* are the only variable that doesn't change. The question is not *Why are some men such trash?* (though if you find out why, please let me know!); the question is, What belief or psychology or hurt inside of *you* causes you to put out that level of vibration? *Please don't let this guy be garbage, please don't let this guy be garbage, please don't let this guy . . .* The vibration is fear, disgust, worry, anxiety—the list of low energy is extensive, and the focus is guy + garbage. The obsession over what you **don't** want will always attract more of the same.

So then in order to manifest what we actually *want* in life . . . we must raise our vibrational level to the vibrational level of what we want.

You want an incredible partner? Then make *yourself* an incredible partner.

You want to attract more joy in your life? Curate joy! Watch funny movies, go to the dog park, do things that make you happy every day.

You want more abundance? Stop living in scarcity.

You want more health? Stop messing with things that make you sick.

Your actions have to match your words. Your energy has to match the level you say you want to be at. You have to live as if the blessing is already upon you, because by the way, blessings always are. There are a million teachers, much smarter than me, who can teach you about this (Wayne Dyer I mentioned earlier and Abraham Hicks are two of my favorite authors on the subject if you want to deep dive), but before you jump into those questions, ask yourself this one: What are you attracting to your life?

Is this real?

Me and the internet.

It's been a tool for exploration, a source of endless free wisdom, and a chance to connect with people. First it was old friends from high school or my kindergarten boyfriend. Later it was women from all around the world.

I became a professional writer because of my access to the internet. I have a podcast for the same reason. I've built an online community and a small business and directed my first short film all thanks to information I found on the internet. I've used the internet to intentionally create content that has helped people, and I've also unintentionally created content that was offensive. I've learned from the internet in a thousand different ways. But I worry that the greatest lesson I've learned from the internet is how to fake a happy life.

I don't mean to say that I haven't been happy. Over the last decade, as social media has exploded, so has my life and my work. I've experienced wonder beyond measure and success that far surpasses anything I could have imagined as a little girl. I have incredible, cherished relationships with my kids. I have beloved friends and family. I get to do work that inspires me. I'm privileged beyond measure, unlike many other mamas raising kids; I don't have to worry about how to pay rent or whether or not I can afford a doctor's bill. I'm blessed beyond belief, and I can point to endless moments of joy along the way. I've been so happy.

But let's be real—I've also been depressed, anxious, livid, lazy, overwhelmed, lost, and sometimes really, truly dull as dishwater.

The internet though, she doesn't seem to want all the in-between parts. She doesn't want the whole story: she wants the highest highs, and she *glories in the lowest lows*. So if you need to utilize the internet to promote your work, your business, your nonprofit, etc., you learn very quickly to show the highlight reel. Because nobody—I don't care how evolved they claim to be—wants to have a global audience of strangers weighing in on the most difficult moments of their life.

It starts off innocuous enough. You have a great hair day, and it's a perfect moment to post a picture on Instagram. Your first (real or fur) baby is born, and you're so proud, you could burst, so you put his pictures on your Facebook. You have a great idea for other people in your industry, so you write a little blog post for LinkedIn. The intention is pure, but the internet doesn't allow innocence to exist for long. Almost immediately, this machine begins to manipulate our behavior.

Whenever you put something out into the world of the internet, you get immediate feedback. You learn very quickly what people like: pictures of family, of your dog, of a great outfit—anything that your followers aspire to will get praise. There's a handful of things that get you more likes than others, and you learn, even if it's unconscious, to craft your content around those likes. *This is so fun*, you think. *I'm finding friends and community who are into what I'm into!*

But sooner or later, you don't have any more dog pictures or baby pictures or it's not a good hair day. You decide to mix things up and tell the internet about another passion of yours. You talk about how you're really into anime or English-style horseback riding or rockabilly music. You tell them about how you're in a pagan folk band or that you're thinking of running for local office or that you tried contouring for the first time, and while you know you're no professional, *it's not too bad, right?*

And what was a seemingly cool space to put yourself out there suddenly becomes something else entirely.

At the very least, this post, which is unlike the other things you've created, won't get as much attention. It gets two likes instead of the twenty that you're used to. And if you weren't wired the way most humans are, that wouldn't matter to you at all. You'd think, *OK, cool, so I have two friends who are into motocross too!*

Alas, poor Yorick! That's not the way you've been groomed to behave.

The internet and its instantaneous feedback have taught you to chase praise and approval. Every single time you paid attention to the likes, retweets, or positive emojis you received, you got a little hit of dopamine. That dopamine is addicting; the digital praise helps to make up for the areas in your real life where you don't feel loved, understood, or supported.

And that's just what happens when the internet *ignores* you and your post. Far more destructive—and far more common with every passing month—is what happens when the comment section finds a reason to make fun of what you created *as their form of creation.*

Do they even think about what they're doing? I ponder this sometimes.

Like, do the internet trolls sit around in the corner of their mom's basement and think, *Let me see if I can write the funniest comment about this guy's first attempt at woodworking.* Or *How many likes can I get for tearing apart this girl's painting?* I assume this is because if your hateful comment can get enough likes, it will make you significant, right? Then maybe you won't feel so badly about your lack of creation, your terror of putting yourself out there, or your super tiny penis.

I follow the most incredible baker on Instagram who makes gorgeous videos of the prettiest sourdough you've ever seen. She uses tiny stork scissors to cut out indentions in the dough and make cool designs. Each video is aesthetically pleasing and set to vibey music. As far as I'm concerned, her work is art—a small, ethereal service to humanity that asks nothing, sells nothing, and is beauty for beauty's sake.

You **would not believe** the hateful things the internet spews in her comments section.

"Get a life, snowflake," they bark at her. "Why would anyone waste so much time this way?" "She's faking it. No way she's actually making that!"

She's baking sourdough, you guys. If sourdough lady gets abused by the internet, what hope is there for the rest of us?

The internet will find a reason to disapprove of anything, of everything, of what you said or *what it thinks you said* or maybe what you didn't say enough of.

You post about how you just signed up for your first half marathon, and lots of friends and family celebrate you . . . but then there's a couple of comments. Your mother-in-law passive-aggressively drops in: *This new generation of women, with its "me time," is just so different. We never would have pursued that with a family to raise.* Next, it's Stephanie, a girl you went to high school with. She adds on, *Oh, I'd love to do something like that, but my priorities are always going to be my children and family. #MomLife*

Never mind that when you last saw Steph, she was wearing a Limp Bizkit T-shirt and smoking chronic out of an apple. Never mind that you have no way of knowing what her priorities actually are or what kind of person she truly is. She's dropped a passive-aggressive grenade into your comments section—basically the internet's version of "Bless your heart"—and publicly shamed you. Since every time you've posted about being a mom you've never received anything but affirmation, this feels shocking. You can't help but worry, *Am I doing something wrong? Is it bad to try long-distance running if it means spending some time away from my middle schooler? Is training for my first race a bad thing?*

What *was* a thrilling challenge for you is now colored by something negative.

Or maybe you post about how you've just started nursing school, and this time, the comment isn't from someone you know; it's from a stranger you've never met. She remarks that it *must be nice* to have all that extra money to take classes when she can barely make ends meet. The stranger doesn't know you or your story. She doesn't know that you saved up for eighteen months to be able to go back to school and that you want to make it a career that will better help you support your daughter. Now you feel like you're in trouble, like you've done something wrong, when really, you were proud of yourself and wanted to share. You think, *Should I explain? Should I defend myself?*

You make a mental note . . . every time you post about school, make sure you explain the whole backstory so you're allowed to publicly acknowledge what you're doing.

If you were raised to be a good girl / people pleaser, the internet teaches you very quickly how to say whatever you're trying to say in a way that will be least offensive—and just so we're clear, everything is offensive to somebody.

Years ago, when I was a food blogger, I mentioned on Facebook that I made my chocolate chip cookies with room-temperature eggs (the butter and the eggs cream together more easily, and the cookie comes out perfect).

I was digitally slaughtered.

The comments were aggressive to the point of crazy. They told me I was going to give people salmonella. They told me I was being irresponsible and spreading dangerous information. One angry comment gave space to another and another. I felt sick to my stomach and so mad at myself for saying the wrong thing. I deleted the post because I figured I had really screwed up big, and I didn't want to upset anyone else.

Now let's just take a quick moment to dig into the psychology of that room-temperature egg post. First of all, ask any good baker about it.

Or better yet, google it.

The advice was right on. But that doesn't really matter here; what matters is that I was just explaining how I *bake cookies*. I didn't take on the patriarchy, propose a solution for how to restructure the Electoral College, share a spoiler, or announce that the dress was blue, not gold.

I wasn't saying anything inflammatory, but I got burned just the same. The whole thing was nonsensical, yet still, twelve years later, there's a part of me that gets anxious just remembering how it felt to get into "trouble" with the internet.

Odds are at least some of you are wondering, *If something caused so much negativity in your life, why didn't you just stop engaging with it?*

Fantastic ponderance!

I kept interacting with the internet for only one reason. My job requires me to do so.

But even if your business or career doesn't ask that of you in any way, the majority of people—especially anyone under thirty—were brought up in a world where social media wasn't just part of life but, in many ways, a substitute for it.

Depression and suicide rates in teenagers have climbed steadily since 2011. You know what happened in 2011? Social media was created. Forty-nine percent of people between eighteen and twenty-five report experiencing anxiety or depression. That's half the people! If this is the first time you're hearing that statistic, I'm guessing it's perhaps because you don't hang out with many younger people.

I've experienced internet-related anxiety as an adult, but imagine what it would be like to have grown up with it. Imagine what it must be like to try to make the internet "happy" ... starting in middle school. Many of you won't have to imagine it because you're watching your children struggle with it now.

In junior high, I had the body composition of a Squishmallow, and my teeth looked like a broken zipper. Imagine me trying to post a picture for the internet's approval. One shudders.

As far as I can tell, making the internet happy involves the following:

1. Creating the best of the best visual of the best of the best life.
2. Saying something interesting, unique, special, smart, funny, witty, or thought-provoking ... but making sure you say it in a way that doesn't upset anyone.
3. If you're a woman, making sure you never show a skill, a talent, or a success without first removing any personal involvement you had it in. It was a *team effort*, you *got lucky*, *would you look at God ...*
4. Choosing a lane! And once you choose that lane, don't ever, for any reason, question it, step outside of it, or evolve away from it. Don't change. Ever. The algorithm won't like you talking about

pottery when you're known as a legal secretary. Also, the internet will use this change as ammunition to dig back into a tweet from 2008 to remind you that you once said *you hated cilantro, but now, you're eating a barbecue chicken pizza with cilantro on it, so you're fake as hell!*

5. Remembering that no matter how much content you feed the internet, it will never be enough. It will always want more, and if you don't feed it at the level to which it's become accustomed, you risk losing its affection entirely. *Better hurry up, you haven't posted since this morning, and people are getting antsy.*

This list is insane. It's an impossible ask—but damn is it easy to get wrapped up in the belief that you *can* do the internet "right"!

I forever got stuck at the very first rule. Capturing the best visual was impossible for me to accomplish without constantly halting my *real life* to show the internet my "best life." I shudder remembering how many times I asked my kids to stop doing something fun so I could take a picture of us doing something fun. I'm so disappointed with myself for every concert I watched through my phone screen so I could show it on my stories instead of actually just enjoying my favorite band. I hate thinking about how much of my work I sped up, sped through, and put into the world without intention because I believed that I had to post and post and post.

I spent a decade living inside the idea that if the internet liked my content today, then my life was good, and if they didn't like my content today—I was bad.

See, that's what's so wild about this vortex of fifteen-second videos and flat lays and comments and likes . . . we begin to believe that who we are on the internet or how we're perceived by the internet is who we really are.

You buy into the hype that a good life is something you can manifest through an Instagram feed. All this teaches us is how to better angle the camera, light the shot, or use editing software to soften our giant pores because we hate how they look.

Real life has one key essential: your presence in it.

If you want your real life to be good, it requires intention and probably therapy. It means getting good sleep and practicing self-care and healing generational trauma. A good life for you might be finally getting a dog, moving to a new city, or apologizing for a past hurt. Real life is often unglamorous and not necessarily pretty enough for your feed without some augmentation . . . but the second you begin to dress up real life to make it pretty for others, it ceases to be about what's real and becomes about what's aesthetically pleasing.

The truth is, the most beautiful, most well received, most widely liked picture you've ever posted is never going to feel as good as the time you laughed with your bestie until your sides hurt. The beautifully curated TikTok of a trip to Italy, timed perfectly to the exact right song, is never going to beat the taste of pistachio gelato on the Spanish Steps or the breathless feeling you had when you saw the ceiling of the Duomo for the first time.

I know this because I experienced life—real life—long before I ever experienced the internet. And when I finally did become sick—spiritually, emotionally, and physically—of trying to be the internet's version of an ideal, it's because I've experienced real life that I was able to navigate back to it.

I'm not suggesting that every part of the internet is bad and there aren't a million beautiful things about how it serves us: that sourdough bread maker, for instance. I *am suggesting* that far too many people (myself included) have fallen into the false belief that our life, our worth, and our potential for joy is locked inside an app on our phone and the opinion of strangers. We've come to accept that the world is hateful and divided because that's what we see in our newsfeeds. We buy into opportunities that turn out to be scams, we accept internet rumors as factual news, and conspiracy theories become gospel so long as the YouTube video they're presented in is well produced.

I don't have the answer for anyone else's life—most days, I feel like I barely have the answers for my own, but I know this much is true: your **real** life is the only thing that's ***really*** **happening to you**.

So the next time you find yourself consuming social media and you feel your energy shift, your vibration lower, or you sense that your mood is getting worse, not better, I want you to ask yourself:

Is this real? Did anything really happen to me just now to make me feel this way? Did anything shift in my real life? Or did I just see something (or see many things) that made me compare myself, that made me judge myself, that made me feel worse? It's possible to put your phone down; look up at the gorgeous, imperfect world around you; and begin to live in it. For real.

What do you *actually* need?

I was thirty-nine the first time I had a panic attack.

Have you all ever experienced one? It's the absolute worst. Let me tell you all about it!

It happened in—of all places—a Paul McCartney concert. One second, I was fine, and the next second, I was splayed on the ground like an abandoned doll.

I was on the floor because our brains don't work super well inside a panic attack. You can't think (or speak!) in whole sentences so your thoughts come at you in simple and intense jumbles, like Brendan Fraser in *Encino Man*. I was so hot—burning alive actually, and my caveman brain screamed: *Floor! Cold maybe! You lie!*

My only goal at that moment was to bring my body temperature, currently hovering somewhere around three hundred degrees, down to a more manageable level.

I'm normally pretty skeeved out by the presence of germs in public places, especially mushing my face into them—but I was desperately trying to cool off, which is also why my brain yelled: *No shoes! Toes on cold floor!*

So just to recap, I'd made it to the walkway outside the floor of the arena before lying down on the floor beside my shoes and socks—my personal downfall accompanied by a jaunty rendition of "Ob-La-Di, Ob-La-Da."

This was not how I imagined I'd experience my first interaction with a Beatle.

From the floor I was staring directly at the long line of people waiting impatiently for overpriced margaritas. More than a few of them stared unabashedly at my demise.

Mortifying.

I'm absolutely positive that everyone who watched me from the concession line that day assumed I was drunk.

But, guys, I wasn't drunk. I was dying.

And even dying, I worried that someone in that line might recognize me: *Is that Rachel Hollis? I guess the Lord giveth and the Lord taketh away . . .*

La-la, how their life goes on . . .

At some point I became aware that my sweet boyfriend was beside me.

Was he with me the whole time?

Did he get worried and come out to find me lying here like roadkill?

Guys, I have no idea.

He kept asking me questions, but I no longer understood English. I'm a caveman, remember? He was Charlie Brown's teacher: wuah wuah wuah wuah. I had zero idea what he was asking me.

Then everything in my entire body sped up and sort of shut down all at once.

I got hotter. My skin was burning me alive. I actually didn't know it was possible to be that hot without frying your brain like those antidrug commercials from the '80s. *This is your brain on drugs.*

I'd sweat through all of my clothes at that point and kept thinking—legitimately considering—taking my shirt off in public.

Obviously I didn't, because of all those concession-stand people staring at me. Even in the midst of a panic attack, an upbringing steeped in modesty still held sway.

Then my caveman thoughts sort of separated from my real thoughts. That separate part of me marveled at the spectacle I was making: *Why am I doing this?*

"You're OK," my boyfriend said. "You're having a panic attack."

Huh? The detached part of me wondered. Why on earth would this happen now?

My first-ever panic attack at almost forty? In the middle of a Paul McCartney concert?? It feels so disrespectful to someone knighted by the queen. But given my body's reaction, either I was having a panic attack, or I'd been poisoned. Since Vizzini hadn't challenged me to a battle of wits over iocane powder, I had to assume the former.

Something in me bristled at my weakness.

I'm stronger than this, that detached voice was now screaming.

To prove it, I tried to sit up, but the world tilted on its axis—the margarita machine everyone was waiting in line for became triplets. I immediately collapsed back down, violently jostling my tenuous equilibrium, which made me feel dizzy.

And then, suddenly, I was desperate.

I was about to have violent diarrhea . . . in my pants . . . in front of the concession stand full of people.

Ob-la-di, Ob-la-da . . .

To be fair, I think it's safe to say that most people would not want to crap themselves in the hall of a concert arena. But, you guys, I am one of the biggest prudes you've ever met! I don't even like other people to hear the sound of me *peeing*!

Pooping my pants in public would be my worst nightmare. Multiplied by one thousand!

I scanned the hallway in a desperate search for a bathroom. Unfortunately, I had no idea how I could get there without crapping myself along the way.

Let's also add into the mix the beautiful man who brought me to that concert was, at that point, still a fairly new relationship. Like, it was so new, I was still regularly shaving my legs. All the way to the top—not just to the knee, guys!

It was bad enough that he had to watch me have a meltdown, but if I did actually lose control of my bowels in front of him? That would be the end of me.

You know those stories of mothers who develop superhuman strength in an emergency and find the ability to hoist a car off their toddler or something? That's the exact kind of willpower it took for me to make it across that arena to the bathroom *while clenching my butt cheeks together and trying not to pass out.*

I didn't even try the ladies' room either (too many innocent bystanders). I went into the family restroom where it was blessedly private and where fluids shot out of every hole in my body like they were escaping from a monster.

I'm embarrassed to tell you, I still didn't have any shoes on. Which means I was barefoot in a public restroom. *insert gagging sound here* The moment I stopped expelling everything from my body, my brain very urgently suggested that I lie down again, this time on the bathroom floor, and go to sleep. *insert even deeper gagging sound*

The bathroom floor of an arena?? That's the kind of contagion exposure you can't come back from. With my last remaining strength, I forced myself to get out of that bathroom before I passed out in a field of *E. coli*. I made it back to my original position in the hallway on the floor beside my shoes—my boyfriend tried to keep me from lying down again, but gravity won.

"I'm so hot," I mumbled. My lips were stuck to my teeth.

"Your temperature is totally normal," he assured me matter-of-factly.

"I feel like I'm dying,"

"You're not dying."

No matter what I said that night, he would calmly but sternly assure me that I was fine. He was adamant to the point of being rude. Caveman brain couldn't understand it—it has the emotional stability of a shelter puppy. Everything my boyfriend said started to sound mean. I felt like I was talking to a stranger. This new guy was completely unlike the man I fell in love with. The man I fell in love with is deeply compassionate and very gentle. This one was (for the first time in our relationship) purposely antagonistic. He kept squeezing my hand really hard in between my index finger and my thumb . . . and it *hurt*.

Through my fog of panic, I started to get a little annoyed.

"You're having a panic attack," he said again. A twenty-plus-year veteran of the music industry, he's spent decades tour managing for rock icons and pop stars and everything in between. He assured me that panic attacks happen to people at concerts all the time. "The lights, the sound, the heat, the crowd. It's really common."

"My heart is pounding so hard."

He felt my pulse. "It's not pounding; the rhythm is exactly right. Honestly, Rachel, you're being a bit dramatic."

My thoughts started to form in full sentences again. Now I was getting truly pissed.

There I was DYING, and he was acting like it was all a big "dramatic" inconvenience for him. I thought of the celebrity he was currently working with. A childish part of me crossed her arms and stamped a foot. *I bet if **he** were right here dying, you'd be a lot nicer to **him**.*

"I can call the EMTs over for you, but they'll want to take you in." At that moment, a security guard walked by. "Hey, brother, how many songs are left before the end?" my soon-to-be ex-boyfriend asked in that maddeningly calm tone.

"Two more, man. Does she need a stretcher?"

Judas looked back at me.

"Two more songs, Rachel. Should they put you on a stretcher?" he asked.

Meaning, in exactly two songs, fifteen thousand people would exit the arena and walk by me there on the floor.

Oh, hell no!

Whatever willpower kept me from ruining my pants would definitely give me the energy to save what was left of my reputation. I hauled myself to my feet, annoyed enough at this jerk-wad to want to huff off but not steady enough on my feet to walk unaided. He held one of my arms and both of my shoes, and we shuffled out, very slowly, into the Dallas night.

When we got back to our hotel room, I collapsed across the bed, unable to move. I was woken a little while later to the sensation of the aforementioned jerk-wad washing my feet.

"Poor darling," he murmured in his beautiful English accent as he methodically cleaned my feet like some biblical character.

"You're nice again." My voice sounded small and weak. "Why were you so mean earlier?"

"Love, I'm sorry. But nothing else was working. You'd lost all your color, and your anxiety was getting worse and worse. I tried talking to you, helping you, cajoling—the only thing I hadn't tried was making you angry. You needed something to break your pattern. In that moment, you didn't need someone to coddle you; you needed someone to challenge you so that you'd snap out of the spiral."

I fell asleep that night deeply bruised, both physically and emotionally.

I've spent most of my life feeling like I've always got to be the strong one in every relationship. I have endless experiences of being asked to take on other people's responsibilities, clean up other people's messes, and try to save those who refuse to save themselves. It was deeply triggering for me to experience a crisis and not find the support I'd expected from my partner.

But I'm not the same person who once stayed in those past unhealthy familial, personal, or romantic relationships. I have grown up since then. I've worked hard to learn to say what I'm feeling, even if I know it will lead to conflict. So the next morning, when I had a clearer head, I brought it up again.

And now, I didn't try to fit my feelings into special packaging. I just said what I was thinking: "I didn't feel supported by you last night when I really needed you."

He sat with my words for a moment. His slow consideration is a hallmark of his thoughtful personality and a big reason he's so successful in his field—I don't think anybody can create a more calming presence and give you clear wisdom the way he can. It's like being in love with Yoda—only this one is way hotter.

"I hear that you didn't feel supported, and I'm sorry. I'd never want you to feel that way. But, darling, would you consider that you were supported very deeply, just in a way you *needed* at that moment, not in the way you *wanted*? Sometimes what you need doesn't come in the form you want it to."

Well, damn.

He was right. The first clear thoughts I remember (well, besides that whole exorcism in the bathroom) were of being annoyed with him. The more I spiraled, obsessing about my heart pounding, the harder it pounded. The more I thought about how hot it was, the hotter I became. I have no idea if I lay on the floor for ten minutes or two hours, but I do know I was getting worse, not better. I really only started to come back to rational thinking in order to argue with him. I was only able to walk out of the arena under my own steam because I was annoyed. I got the support from him that I needed, the kind that would actually help me, instead of being cosseted the way I would have preferred.

There are times in life when you need care and love and back rubs and kisses. You long for someone to *see you* and the hardship you've walked through. You wish they would pamper and maybe even baby you a little, but you're too afraid to ask or don't think you deserve it.

Then there are other times in life where even though it's the kind of support you want, it's not actually what you *need* to snap you out of the fog you've been living in. Sometimes you need someone to apply a little pressure to a point of tension, like when he squeezed that spot next to my thumb so hard it hurt. Sometimes you need someone to challenge your thoughts because they're no longer serving you.

I can't get up off this floor.
Yes. You can and you will.

My heart isn't strong enough.
Your heart is strong; the rhythm is exactly right.

This is the end of me.
Silly rabbit, you're just getting started.

So what if, just for perspective, you ask yourself what you **need** in this season of life? Not what you want but what you *actually* *need*? Both from other people and also from yourself. The answer might just surprise you. The answer might not soothe your current moment; in fact, there's a good chance what you actually *need* might not be soothing at all. But it could be healing. It could be helping. It could be exactly what you need to break the pattern you're trapped inside of.

Who would you be without your fear?

A few years back, on the very first day of January, I made a life-altering decision . . . only, I didn't know it at the time.

I was utterly fed up with the way I was feeling. I'd hit my threshold of pain. I desperately wanted something to change. What my problems were and what I decided to implement seemed so far apart as to not be connected at all. Weirdly, that seemingly insignificant choice healed so many parts of my life. And it all started with a confession on a blustery cliff in England.

Dramatic stuff.

In order to understand the state I was in on that particular day, I first have to explain where I was emotionally.

Three weeks earlier, I'd suffered a miscarriage as I entered my second trimester of pregnancy. It had utterly decimated me.

But back to this day on the cliff, on the first day of a new year.

I was in England with my boyfriend. Remember the human Yoda from the last chapter? Well, we'd come to Cornwall to see his family and friends for the new year. When you're in love with someone who has an entire life and world of loved ones in another country, a trip like that (our first to celebrate the holidays with his family) is common. But making that trip—one we'd planned months before—when I was so hormonal and distraught was an absolute nightmare for me. And for him too, as I now more fully realize.

I was meeting most of his dearest friends for the first time. So there I was trying to look my best and be funny and cool and impressive—while still bleeding from a miscarriage. I didn't want to be there. I wanted to crawl into bed and wake up when my heart stopped hurting so much, but life doesn't work like that. Life kept right on going, and I needed to as well. In retrospect, that trip was actually really good for me. I'd already spent one full week in bed. Then it was the Christmas holiday with my kids, which forced me to get it together and make it special for them regardless of how I was feeling. Once they left to spend time with their dad, I went to England for this previously planned trip. That time kept me busy, which was likely a godsend even if I'd much rather have been wallowing.

By January first though, I was at the end of my ability to entertain other people. I felt deeply low. Low in spirit, low in energy—my life-force was utterly depleted. Which was made infinitely worse by the fact that January first is historically one of my favorite days of the year. I freaking *love* New Year's Day!

I love envisioning the future and planning out goals. I love a New Year's Eve journal session, followed by a New Year's Day vision board party—*remember my telling you about my friends gathering for Vision Cast?!* I love daydreaming about what the year might hold. I adore all that frothy possibility.

But on this particular New Year's Day, in that particular mental state—the only future I could envision was dark and sad. Which just made me sadder.

I was sad about what had happened and then sad that I was sad. Oy.

Once we got to Europe, my sweet boyfriend was infinitely

patient, but like I assume with most partners, he was fairly lost as to how to help me in a grief he couldn't fully understand. His answer was lots of hugs mixed with cooking and baking delicious things so I would eat—which, by the way, is just about as good a support as you could dream of under the circumstances. But the thing he was pretty adamant about, regardless of whether or not I felt like it, was taking walks. Every day. *Let's just move a little*, he'd say. *Let's just get your face out in the sunshine. Let's get some fresh air.*

Y'all. I *hated* those walks.

I was sad and miserable, but at least indoors, I could be sad and miserable *and warm*. We were on the coast of England at the end of December. It was freezing and windy, and the skies were perpetually gray. The weather matched my mood perfectly.

I didn't want to go outside. I didn't want to take walks. But I also knew how hard he was trying to help me even as my moods swung back and forth like an emotional teeter-totter. I was either crying or being a bitch . . . or crying because I was being bitchy, and this man was doing his best, just like I was doing my best (even if it was the worst!), and to top it all off . . . *he was right!*

I knew that it was good for me and my emotions to get outside and move around. *Move your body, change your mind.* I've said that at least a hundred times myself. I've had it printed on a workout towel! I knew it would help. So even if I hated it, I did it.

But in my head, I cursed every step we took on our daily walks around Cornwall . . . which would have been a charming English hamlet if I didn't hate the world.

So we walked. Every day, blast him.

And New Year's Day was no exception. He cajoled me into taking yet another frigid trek to the shore, which is how I found myself on the jagged seaside cliffs staring at the turbulent sea.

I'm not sure how long we stood there while I wallowed in

self-pity and he worried about how much I was struggling. I was searching for something—*any idea*—that would help me feel better.

If I could just have one *believable* goal, I thought to myself, no matter how small, I knew it would help my enneagram type 3 / Capricorn personality find a little hope.

I was deep in my head and swirling around a central thought: *How can I heal? What will make me feel better?* Without any conscious thought about what the answer was, I opened my mouth, and the most unexpected sentence fell out.

"I'm so tired of being afraid all the time."

He looked at me with confused compassion.

"What do you mean?"

I wasn't sure what I meant. I'd never, *ever* thought of myself as fearful. I do big, terrifying things all the time. I chase down massive goals and push myself outside my comfort zone on the regular. I'm not afraid to speak with anyone, no matter how fancy or impressive. I've met my heroes, all larger-than-life personalities, and I managed to have mature, intelligent conversations with them without my voice shaking once. I told you earlier how I bombed in front of Oprah's audience and how she continued to speak with me afterward onstage? Well, here's what else you need to know about that night: afterward she *visited me in my dressing room* because—I'm hypothesizing here—she's a goddess and knew the visit would be a highlight of my life (which it is!). My dressing room was roughly the size of a large freezer, which means I was *mere inches* away from a deity, and yet somehow I managed to be totally composed—even when I noticed that she was wearing her divine tiger's-eye earrings featured in ***at least*** one hundred episodes of her show (only the true fans would recognize them). *Even then* I kept it together! Because I'm brave.

I'm brave, right? I asked myself on that New Year's Day.

I'm brave, but only in ways that feel safe to me, my inner wisdom answered back. I'm brave by someone else's definition because standing onstage or chasing down a dream . . . those things aren't really scary to me. But little stuff, the kind of things that other people don't bat an eyelash at? **That kind of stuff is terrifying.** I shy away from so many things that seem fun because while I was courageous in some ways, I was a pretty big weenie in others.

I am a weenie about being cold—which cancels out my visits to any chilly climate.

I'm a weenie about feeling physically out of control—which eliminates skateboarding, bike riding, roller blading, skiing, surfing . . . even though several of those were things I loved doing as a kid.

I'm a weenie about certain animals—most reptiles and small insects. I'm a weenie about heights and mountains and how much it hurts your fingers to learn to play guitar. Basically, if it's uncomfortable or I'm not used to it, I find a way to get out of it.

I was shocked to discover that I was such a weenie, but I'd never once noticed because none of my fears seemed to be holding me back. But here I was, at the lowest of the low points in my life, and some part of me was absolutely sick of it.

I didn't want to be this way anymore! Never mind the fact that I was a disaster and there were probably one hundred things I should be taking on before all my random fears . . . I was resolute. *I'm so tired of being afraid all the time!*

What I lacked in motivation I made up for intention. I decided right then, in that moment, that I'd become brave—not just in some areas but all over, every part of me, fully courageous. I had no idea what to do next, so I did what I always do in that instance . . . I asked the universe for help.

Please help me learn to be brave, I prayed.

I swear, at that exact moment, my love got a text. Everyone back at the house we'd rented with his friends had decided to do a polar plunge. To celebrate the new year, they were going to jump in the Atlantic, which on that day was a balmy forty-two degrees. They were asking if he wanted to go with.

Nobody asked if I wanted to go—they knew better.

But so does the universe.

It knows better. When you ask it to help you be brave, it doesn't magically make you a certain way . . . it provides you with the opportunity to practice bravery.

"I'm in!" I told him.

"Wait, what?" He grinned. "You're going to jump in the ocean with us?"

"Yes! Now let's go, before I change my mind."

I walked back to our rental with conviction. I hadn't actually brought a bathing suit with me on the trip (why would I?), so I wore my giant black period panties and a decades-old sports bra. The whole way down to the beach—wrapped in at least eighteen layers—I mentally prepared myself to take off my clothes on the blustery, freezing beachfront. Never mind the water. I couldn't even contemplate that yet. I was just trying to figure out how to get undressed.

A voice guided me: *Don't think, just do.*

And so I did.

There is a video of me that day, shocking everyone by stripping down to my skivvies on the rocky shore and walking directly into the slate-gray ocean without stopping. Once there, I screamed like I was being murdered, dunked myself up to my neck (still not getting my hair wet, thank you very much!), and ran back out. I shook violently while trying to get redressed, but once I was back in my parka, *I swear*, something was different.

I had certainly done scary things in my adult life, but never with stoicism.

I'd usually whined or built up to it or freaked out. I'm a verbal processor by nature, and I always thought talking about the things I was scared of would help me do them. Walking into the water without hesitation and without any narration on my part was something new.

I was being brave for *myself*, not so that anyone else would think I was brave.

It was entirely new, and as unbelievable as it sounds, I felt like I'd matured a lifetime in that single choice. It makes absolute sense to me now. I'm convinced we can exponentially change our life in a single moment just by doing something we didn't believe we were capable of.

I call it the Holy Shit Moment.

As in, *Holy shit, I can't believe I just did that!!* Between one breath and the next, you change the way you see yourself: *I can't believe **I** just ran a marathon without dying! I can't believe **I** just asked out a stranger! I can't believe **I** just got a tattoo!* You accomplish something you thought was just for "other people," and it's impossible to go back to who you believed you were before.

In that moment, wearing wet underwear on a beach in Cornwall, I made a decision. I would spend the entire year having as many *Holy Shit Moments* as I could. I committed to spending the next twelve months doing things that terrified me.

What happened as a result was a kind of recovery of spirit that could only be divine.

It turns out, things that fall under the banner of "terrifying" also fall under the banner of "That would be impossible for me."

The kind of thing you see someone do and think, *Wow! That's amazing, but I could never ...* That's the magic. That's the special sauce. That's the *it-will-change-your-whole-life-if-you-do-it* kind of thing. During that year, whenever I saw something and my immediate reaction was "No way!" I forced myself to go.

I went zip-lining and skydiving. I ran a marathon *without any training* (and not only did I not die, but I finished a few minutes faster than the marathon I trained six months to accomplish!). I went freediving with sharks, no cage included! I climbed a mountain. I bonded with a neon tiger while doing ayahuasca—I guarantee I was the only mother of four on that psychedelic retreat. I learned to ski by falling down all sorts of snowy mountains—I absolutely loved it. It's become one of my most beloved hobbies. I surf now too—not well or anything, but it fulfills all my *Blue Crush* fantasies and makes me feel *so cool.* I learned to play guitar and write music . . . I'm pretty terrible at those too, but damn, I went ahead and did it anyway. I swam in the ocean (getting my hair wet!) more in that year than in the previous thirty-nine combined. I talked more to strangers and held more compassion for myself and others. By doing scary things nobody ever saw on my social media, I learned so damn much about myself and who I really am.

I realize now, I wasn't tired of being afraid—I was tired of my fears keeping me from living my life more fully. I'm sure this surfaced when it did because anytime you experience trauma, it stirs up all the trauma you've lived through before. The terrified part of you cautions you to play it small and safe so you won't experience pain like this again. Fear accumulates. You don't know what big, scary experiences might be on the horizon, so you start fearing imaginary things. At least that's how it happened for me.

After a year of doing scary stuff, I became aware of two really surprising things. The first is that there really are two kinds of fear.

1. Clear and present danger of a very **real** threat. If an ax murderer is chasing you or a mountain lion just showed up on

your hiking trail, the fear you're feeling is a good thing; it's 160,000 years of evolution working to keep you alive.

2. Imaginary fear. This is the kind of fear we create by dreaming up *what might happen*. This includes anything you've never done, places you've never gone, conversations you've never had, and people you don't know.

The second thing I learned is that while the first kind of fear is (for the most part) a good thing, *that second kind of fear?* The fear of *what might happen*? It's fake news. Not only is it fake news, but it's controlling your life.

Anything you're curious about or interested in but don't pursue because of *what might happen* is **you allowing your fear to control you**. But you created that fear, which means you can destroy it.

By facing my made-up fears (over and over again), I desensitized myself to inaction caused by my imagination. I still get scared sometimes, but I treat it like the skydiving instructor who helped me jump tandem. I was scared when we were still on the ground, but as we approached fourteen thousand feet and I was *petrified*, he acknowledged my fear while adjusting our harness. As we moved closer to the door, he commiserated aloud, "It is scary. You just gotta do it though, right?"

And then he jumped out of the plane.

And since I was wearing him like a backpack, I was suddenly freefalling through the sky.

That's how you have to face your fears: head on.

Take every scary thought you have about the thing you want to do, lay them end to end, give 'em a good look ... and do it anyway. Because you're brave.

What's bigger, your dreams or your excuse?

If you've never pushed through the unique slog that it is to write a book, then you might not know how much it sucks. But let me tell you (or reassure you if you're new to writing and worried that perhaps something is wrong with you because every writing session is hard), it *always* sucks.

Good news though: I woke up this morning feeling great—even more exciting, I woke up this morning actually looking forward to sitting down in front of my computer. I was fully ready to stack one word on top of another in order to hit today's word count.

This is the eleventh book I've written, and the process of writing *never* gets easier.

There are easy sessions locked in flow where the words pour out. There are moments of excitement when you feel as if, even in the first draft, you've connected the dots in a way that's clever or funny or insightful. But writing days like that are the exception, not the rule. To get to the end of a completed manuscript—even if it's a flaming pile of garbage—takes *wild* tenacity and maybe a small amount of masochism.

But like I said, this morning I woke up feeling excited about the work—or at least energized enough to jump right into it. It's holiday break, so my writing session has the added benefit of being trimmed by twinkle lights and a prime view of Belle (our Elf on the Shelf) dangling from the ceiling. It seems at some point in the night, she constructed a swing out of markers and ribbon, hung it from a rafter (which must have been difficult because she's so short), and will spend the day perched above us all. Tonight, I'm sure she'll come up with another extravagant adventure to delight the children in the morning. She never runs out of ideas and never, ever wishes she could take a night off from all the holiday merriment in order to laze about with a crisp glass of dry white wine and a proper binge of Dan Levy's outfits on *The Big Brunch*.

I woke up early this morning—but sadly so did my five-year-old. *How can they sense it, y'all? How do they know when we wake up?* I can ninja myself through the house completely soundless, like I'm trying to avoid those monsters in *A Quiet Place*, and she still somehow knows. I didn't step on any of the locations where the hardwood squeaks. I made my coffee with the quiet precision of a brain surgeon so as not to jostle or knock into anything that might wake her up on the other side of our home. I didn't even *breathe* a single decibel above the natural room tone. But no sooner had I taken a sip of coffee than I looked over to discover my five-year-old staring at me silently like the *Children of the Corn*. After a violent double-take and the confirmation that she was not, in fact, the ghost of some Victorian child, I was resigned to my fate. She just bogarted my early morning productivity.

Le sigh.

But plans change, and parents are *hella good* at rolling with the punches. So since long before the sun came up, I've been making eggs and putting together unicorn puzzles. I do this between sips of coffee that never stays warm long enough for me to enjoy an entire cup at the right temperature. We got through the morning melee and the same but decidedly less intense routine with her ten-year-old brother a couple of hours later. At some point, everyone seemed settled long enough for me to steal away to the kitchen table for this writing session I woke up so excited about. I was going to write about how fear holds us back from pursuing something bigger and better for our lives—it was going to be fantastic!

I set myself up at the little table in the kitchen with a bottle of water and some lukewarm coffee. Before I could even open my laptop, my daughter was beside me.

"What are you doing, Mommy?"

I'm immediately anxious. Being noticed by a five-year-old when you're trying to take a little time for yourself is like being noticed by a great white while swimming on your period—dead in the water.

"I'm going to do a little writing," I told her. "Could you go back in the TV room and finish the movie? Or you can play in the living room so you can see me the whole time."

Noah would prefer to live her entire existence physically within ten inches of everyone she loves, but in a pinch, a visual will do.

"No, Mommy. I want to sit by you."

The part that was anxious just got joined by a part that's angry. *I was so excited to write this morning,* a voice in my head says. *This book is due soon! And how do these kids think I make money to pay for our life?* This voice is more petulant.

The mature part of my mind calmly reminds me that Noah is five and that she only wants to be around me—it's so little to ask. *It goes so fast,* the voice of maturity adds. *Someday she won't want to be around you like this.*

Blargh.

"OK, why don't you grab your markers and some paper, and you can draw beside me. I can't talk to you while I work though, OK?" She's already run off for art supplies, and in the two minutes it takes her to go and come back, I've started on my first sentence.

There are three kinds of people . . .

I was about to make some profound, sweeping generalizations, y'all.

When she runs back in the room and starts to slam accessories on the table in order to set up her own station, I had to take some calming breaths.

I know I'm not supposed to say that. I'm *supposed* to tell you that it was so precious to have her beside me "working" and that as soon as we settled into a little rhythm (just two gals being creative!), I realized the error of my ways and counted my blessings.

But what actually happened was that I felt pissed.

All I wanted was an hour of time to write—and not even an hour of time luxuriously typing away at a hip little coffee shop. No, I was trying to eke out an hour of writing time while my five-year-old put stickers on every piece of furniture in the house and my fifth grader watched a movie on a volume level typically reserved for octogenarians. I was trying to fit my hopes and dreams into real life, which you usually *have* to do if you ever want those hopes and dreams to manifest. And even crammed into the smallest of creative confines, *I still had to accommodate everyone else.*

And let's be honest—that's parenting.

Not in total, obviously.

Lots of parts of parenting can be pretty flipping magical, but . . . there's also a massive loss of personal autonomy you can't properly understand until it's already gone. Not to mention your sense of self (or even the time to figure out who your "self" actually is) seems to slip away along with your ability to remember what you walked into the kitchen to get.

I accept it. But it's still super frustrating sometimes. It *still* makes me feel grouchy and cheated on occasion. I still have to try not to let my frustration spill out of my mouth and into a therapy session my daughter will have someday when she's in her twenties.

I took a deep breath and then another. I told her to, yes, go ahead and set up shop here next to Mommy. Which she did. While almost immediately dropping a box of art supplies on my bare foot. That box somehow landed on the exact right nerve to send an electric shock through my body and a curse word flying out of my mouth—under my breath, but still. It started with an *F* and ended with an *-uck*, and then . . . I just gave up.

I slammed my computer shut and walked out of the room. I went into the living room and counted to ten, and when she followed me there too, I tried not to cry in front of her.

Can I be real with you guys?

It feels so goddamn impossible sometimes.

Raising four kids and working full time and then trying to come up with a creative thought or an interesting way to get a point across in the chapter of a book—preferably an example I haven't used before. When I'm tired or hormonal or close to burnt out, it feels *impossible*. It feels impossible for me, and I'm not worried about paying my bills. I'm not stressed about whether or not my kids are living in a dangerous neighborhood or concerned about where we'll sleep tonight. It feels impossible for me, and my most basic needs are met.

So what does it feel like when your most basic needs aren't met?

A different kind of impossible, but one that's no less true for the person who experiences it. No matter who you are, or where you live, or what your background, this is a universal truth: the hardest thing that's ever happened to you is the hardest thing that's ever happened to you. Your hard thing doesn't diminish because someone else has experienced a situation that's worse. With empathy you can look at someone else's lived experience and understand cerebrally that it must have been brutal for them to endure. But the pain of your parent's divorce when you were twelve doesn't diminish simply because someone else lost a parent when they were nine. Hardship isn't a competition. Inside trauma, nobody wins.

What's hard for you is hard for you.

Ideally, as you move through challenges and push outside of comfort zones and keep going because you must . . . ideally, you become more resilient. Grittier. But at any given moment, most of us have an easily accessible and very good justification for why our dream is freaking impossible to pursue.

"No excuses" looks good on a muscle tee at the gym and is a powerful slogan for the people who've adopted it as a mantra.

But of course there are excuses.

Really freaking *good* excuses. Legitimate reasons for why you don't have the time/energy/resources/connections/support to pursue the dream of your heart. In fact, your excuse is so legitimate, nobody will blame you for giving up on your goal.

Nobody except your heart. Nobody will blame you, except your ten-year-old self who's been dreaming about this thing for thirty-seven years and keeps waiting for you to make it realized. Nobody will blame you, except your ninety-two-year-old self who will look back on life with regret and know that they could have contributed more.

But it won't take you until you're ninety-two to have regrets, will it? You'll regret it long before then. You regret it now. You already have regrets about wasting your precious energy on stupid things that don't actually matter. You already know in your heart you've got more to give. You already *know*.

But every time you start doing your work, taking your steps, walking in faith—*every time* those damn justifiable excuses pop right up again. Something's gotta give. Something *will* give.

Either you'll find a way to push past the very legitimate reasons you have for staying right here in your comfort zone—you'll push past them and surprise yourself with the incredible things you're capable of.

Or you'll live a life that's just *good enough*.

Good but not great.

Good but not exceptional.

Good but not who you know you were born to be.

Your excuses are real, but so is your potential. The question you've got to ask yourself is, What's bigger: my excuse or my dream?

When I think about all of the times I should have given up over the last forty years, it's sort of a wonder to me that I'm still here trying to figure out how to live this life. When I think of how many times my world has been flipped upside down by pain or grief or personal failure, it's enough to make me feel totally worthless.

And yet here I am, stacking these words on top of one another in the hopes that they might be helpful to someone reading them now.

The great excuses I've had to disempower me along the way? Legion. The excuses I've got now? Not as hard as I once faced, but damn, trying to be a good mama and pursue a creative passion feels daunting as hell most of the time.

It might tickle you to know that as I edit this chapter, nearly two years after I first wrote it, I'm sitting beside my daughter Noah (now seven) on an airplane . . . and it wasn't until we reached cruising altitude that I realized her head is *crawling* with lice. I had no preparation for this. No clue how to handle it. Lice? At fifty thousand feet??

I tried to contain it—I put her hair in a bun. Were they on me now? Probably. Every time she aggressively scratched her head, I was sure we'd be discovered. I'm also terrified of catching them, so I partially leaned into the aisle and sat like that for the entire four-hour flight. What do you do in that situation? Y'all, I have no idea, but you know what I did?

I kept her away from others and aggressively sanitized the seats in our aisle with hand-sanitizing wipes every fourteen seconds.

And I worked on this book.

There were seasons when the very justifiable reasons for not pursuing my goals won out. But the dream? It's always there, burning in my heart like a fire. No matter what's happened to me, it can't be snuffed out. My dream is bigger than my excuse.

And so I go again.

I take a breath and count to ten and write this book a couple of paragraphs at a time because that's all life will allow me for today. I decide that a clunky, disjointed pursuit of my dream is better than no dream at all.

What about you?

I'm positive you've got some pretty good rationale for why you're not giving as much effort as you know you can. You've got some seriously incredible reasons for why it's harder for you, why the dream your heart came up with is too big, why you're not the "right person" to pull it off. You're justified.

But why on earth would you let that stop you?

Would you sign up for this again?

I was feeling very overwhelmed by things at work. At the time, my small business that began as a *little-engine-that-could* had turned into a runaway train. The mini but mighty team of six I started with had become sixty employees in the span of eighteen months. On the one hand, that kind of growth feels so exciting! After working at this business for most of my adult life, it was incredible to watch it finally take off. On the other hand, when a business—and the livelihood of its employees—is contingent on you . . . that becomes, at least for me, a nearly debilitating amount of pressure.

The company was a monolithic force in my life, a machine that constantly required more. More energy, more resources, more money, more time—no matter how much I fed it, it was always hungry. I kept thinking if I could just get through this launch . . . if we could just get past the last quarter . . . if we could only hit this new revenue goal, ***then***, then things would calm down.

Quick side note that has nothing to do with this chapter's theme: I am years removed from this experience, and here's what I now know is true. Believing that all that's standing between you and a better life is just getting over the next hurdle?

That's a lie.

That mentality is a myth. Like believing that we'll start our diet "tomorrow," the training "tomorrow," the study "tomorrow." Why do we believe that some mythical future version of ourselves will have the willpower, energy, drive, or determination our present self doesn't currently have? It's called projection bias. That's when the current version of you makes a forecast *as you are now* about how you'll behave differently in the future. Only you're not taking into account that future you will have their own share of hardships and challenges to overcome. This is especially brutal when present you makes decisions today that will be your future self's problem later. Like the extra margarita you order when you should tap out, a ballooning interest rate you signed on for when you bought your condo, or that time Michael Scott agreed to send all those kids to college assuming he'd be rich by the time they grew up.

You know what's just beyond that hurdle you're facing? Another hurdle.

Right past that big launch or project? There will be another and another. Life doesn't get better by *surviving* your current circumstances. Life gets better by *changing* the things you don't like about your current circumstances.

But I didn't understand that yet. Back when my company was expanding so rapidly, I thought the reason all that pressure felt so hard was that I wasn't a strong enough leader. That's the achiever in me—a long (and fairly toxic) bit of wiring makes me believe that if something is hard, it must be because I haven't worked hard enough to figure it out. So I tried to solve this problem the way I always do: I researched.

I researched up and down and sideways on how to be a better leader and better run a company and better manage a team. That multiyear obsession with reading everything I could about how to be a great boss gave me a wealth of information and insight, but there was one single moment of clarity that struck me like lightning. I've applied this insight to business, friendship, and romantic relationships. It's helped me slow down my yeses and speed up my nos. It's a hell of a litmus test for figuring out what to do next, and it's sort of impossible to lie to yourself once you know the right question to ask.

I was watching a YouTube video, and this man (a management guru whose name I truly wish I could tell you, but it was an old-school training video from the '90s, and I have no memory of who he was) was laying out how to grow your team at work and better assess their current skills. Then he dropped this bomb.

"Knowing what you know now about this employee, would you still hire them again today?"

Bro.

If that doesn't punch you in the face with some reality, then maybe you don't have employees. Let's test it out on other relationships. Think about the friends you hang out with, your husband, wife, girlfriend, the club you're a part of... ask this question about each one of them in turn. Knowing what you know today, would you sign up for this again?

Don't overthink it or try to process it or be logical, just go with your gut. What's the first truth that pops into your mind?

Would you still join that group of friends? Would you start a relationship with her again? Would you commit to that project with them?

Please note, I didn't suggest that you erase the past, the work, the good times you've had or anything that came out of the relationship (like your kids). I asked if you, *as you are today*, knowing who *they are today*, would make the decision to move forward **from this point in time**.

Would you sign up for this again?

If you answered no about anyone you are still currently in a relationship with, then may I kindly ask, *What the hell are you doing?*

What we're doing—typically—is staying in something that's no longer right, that no longer works, that's no longer a fit for where we are today.

We do this because we're loyal. We do this because we don't want to hurt anybody. We took responsibility at some point in time, and we've also convinced ourselves that they'll drown if we're not there to keep them afloat. We do this because we keep hoping they'll change. We do this because confrontation makes us feel panicky. We do this because we don't want to be the bad guy. We do this because we're terrified of what other people will say if we step off this approved path.

There's a whole host of reasons we do this, but I'm not sure that knowing why we're blocked from making change is as important as understanding that we are.

Because if you know that you wouldn't choose this person, this career, this particular life path again, that knowing may be painful, but damn, at least you begin to better know *yourself*. Better a painful understanding of who you really are than a catatonic acceptance of life as is simply because you're too far in to turn back now. There's no such thing as "too far in" to choose another path or take a machete to the overgrown jungle that surrounds you on all sides. Get yourself to a place you'd *rather* be, because, y'all, *life is hard either freaking way*. Better a hard that you choose for yourself than one you slowly disappear inside of out of fear.

I had a friend who was unhappy in her career, her life, and her marriage—justifiably so in every instance. She'd left the career of her dreams in New York and moved back to her conservative hometown because of the pressure of her very traditional family who believed that at almost thirty, she should be married and pregnant already. She settled with a man well below her—vibrationally, intellectually, and ambitiously—but the match made her parents happy, and I think she believed she could force herself to enjoy it. Like many women do, she followed that marriage with children, and in order to be a good mama, she took a job she hated—outside her dream industry—not because it would fulfill her but because it would accommodate the near full parental responsibility she now bore as the mother in a traditional town while her husband worked on his own career dreams. With each passing year, she grew less animated, less vibrant, completely unlike the young woman I'd first met. Years later, her husband cheated on her and she called me for advice. It was clear that they hadn't been happy for a while—and so I finally just asked if she was sure she wanted to stay in this thing that wasn't good for anyone involved.

"People who get divorced are selfish," she told me. "It's like they only care about what *they* need or how they want life to go. I'd feel like such a bitch. I'm not that kind of person."

Oh, you guys, *I am*.

I am *that* bitch.

I wasn't at the time. Back then I remember feeling really awful about what she was going through but also trusting her opinion. *Yes*, I thought, *choosing to leave your marriage would be selfish*.

Never mind that he'd cheated, never mind that they didn't even seem to like each other, never mind that after over a decade together, they were both miserable. She had been indoctrinated in the same ideology that I was: Girl, whatever you do, **don't be bad**.

Bad as defined by your family of origin. Bad as prescribed by your religious upbringing. Bad as in the opposite of the kind of person we'd been brought up to believe we *should* be.

I spent a lot of time in that headspace—I spent decades

*should*ing myself before I escaped. I can't even tell you that the journey away from that belief system came on the other side of some huge spiritual awakening. It wasn't a book I read or a conference I went to or a therapist that helped me take control of my life. It was a seismic shift that occurred between one breath and the next.

Inhale.

I can do this, I can carry this load for us all, I can be who they want me to be.

Exhale.

I can't do this, living this way feels like dying, I am not this person.

With that exhale I made a decision to change my whole life.

I didn't know it at the time, but I wouldn't just be changing my life; I'd be changing my career, my community, and the nature of the work I do. Never in my wildest dreams did I imagine the backlash for that decision. The fourteen years of work I'd put in as an entrepreneur had been quickly eaten up by a brand made much more palatable when I did that work alongside a man. Being a good wife was the public preference, and when I chose to stop being that, I was no longer acceptable to some.

I wish I could tell you that I met that criticism with aplomb. I wish I could tell you that I shrugged it off as the opinion of strangers who didn't actually know my circumstances and so it didn't matter to me. I wish I could tell you I remained plucky and optimistic and used it as momentum to go have torrid affairs with every single member of the Avengers and at least two professional athletes. Sadly, though, the breakthrough for me took much longer. I found the courage to leave my marriage long before I found the courage to accept what people thought of me for making that decision.

It took me at least a year to fully accept that I'd done something "bad" and I was at peace with whatever people wanted to think about my choices. In fact, the real acceptance didn't come until I asked myself this question again:

If I had to do it all over again, knowing what I know now—knowing how bad it would get, how awful both strangers and loved ones would respond, how much pain it would cause me and my children—would I do all of it again?

In a heartbeat.

At the time I only knew that something about my marriage and my partner felt very wrong to me on the deepest level. Hindsight has shown me that for years, I was sensing things I didn't have a frame of reference for. It makes me sad to realize how long I ignored my intuition because of a lifetime taught to value others' opinions over my own.

Eventually I made the right decision for me and my children, but it wasn't because I finally had all of the information. It was because I finally had enough courage to face this truth: I wouldn't sign up for it again. I didn't need to know the whole truth yet. I didn't need to have a proper explanation for everyone who would ask me why. The only thing keeping me in my marriage was fear. All the fears I had around what would happen if I didn't stay were finally outweighed by what would happen if I did.

I made the decision to leave because this life, *this is all we get*. It's way too freaking precious and fleeting to waste it just because you've "invested too much time."

If this job/partner/friend was the right choice for you, you wouldn't be constantly questioning whether or not it was. If this was your forever path, you wouldn't answer no when asked if you'd start down it again.

What would you love to forget to remember?

Can I tell you about my most embarrassing moment? It's been years, but it still mortifies me so much that whenever the memory pops into my head, I turn the color of hot house tomato. I always laugh at the hilarity of the remembrance and am equally so self-conscious I could almost die.

It was early 2021, and we were still deeply inside of pandemic rules. This made a night out not impossible but definitely less fun as a proposition. It was a dear friend's birthday weekend, and we decided to celebrate with a night in. I gathered at her house with a group of other friends and—this is an important bit—a coworker of mine and her husband. They were inside the bubble with us because of work, making us all at least close enough to share an evening with.

We ordered Thai food and made cocktails, and after too much of both, we thought it would be fun to go on Clubhouse, which was wildly popular at the time.

If you're not familiar with that platform, it was essentially an app for live podcasts. Anyone anywhere in the world could start talking on any subject and then anyone anywhere in the world could join their "room" and listen in. I had signed up for the app to test it out and almost immediately (thanks to my podcast listeners) had a lot of followers regardless of the fact that I hadn't posted anything yet. I mention this salient point because I want you to understand that this embarrassing moment of mine was about to go down in front of a large crowd of strangers rather than the handful of friends I was sharing the evening with.

That night I decided to try Clubhouse for the first time and enlisted the equally buzzed birthday girl to do a spur-of-the-moment podcast with me. Everyone gathered around the center island of her kitchen, and we hit the "Go Live" button and started chatting. Almost immediately there were thousands of people listening regardless of the fact that we weren't really talking about anything in particular. *Thousands.* It was so cool! We could just hit a button and get a podcast episode without a ton of effort—I was already planning all of the ways I'd incorporate this into my actual show.

I loved the experience so much, I suggested we "take a caller." This was a very cool feature that allowed us to take questions live from one of the audience members who was listening in.

The caller we selected at random was a woman asking us advice on how to navigate life and a career. As she was talking, my friends and I (and the thousands of listeners) were straining to hear her better. I remember vividly how I leaned farther over the counter to get closer to the phone, and—with ZERO warning—my body betrayed me and released the biggest, loudest fart I've ever heard.

Me. I did that.

Before that moment, I had literally never farted in front of anyone in my entire life. Since that moment, I never have again. I don't even like *the word* fart. I'm stressed just typing it out. It's the rudest thing I can imagine. I have so many friends (and teenage sons) who do it all the time, and even when *they* do it, I'm embarrassed. So when the sound came from my body, I literally froze. It was so loud and offensive (like a whoopie cushion being crushed) that I couldn't really connect that I was the one who did it.

The same girlfriends gathered around that center island had teased me *for years* because I'd never farted in front of anyone, so when they heard it, they lost their minds. They were laughing so hard they couldn't breathe. Two of them literally dropped to the floor like they'd been shot. My coworker and her husband straight-up **pretended it didn't happen**—because, keep in mind, the woman on Clubhouse is still talking.

Y'all, that app was audio only.

That means that while that sweet woman shared her story (which made her little avatar icon vibrate along with the soundwaves), *my microphone icon* suddenly (and aggressively) vibrated with the soundwaves of a fart noise.

I'm literally dying. I can't believe I'm telling you this story.

I joined my girlfriends on the floor. I couldn't catch my breath because of how hard I was laughing, and my coworker's husband, who had no formal training (thank you, Jason!), grabbed my phone, introduced himself to the woman, and finished the conversation with her while my friends and I had to hide in a closet to muffle the sounds of our cackling. If any of you were in the session that day and you wondered why I didn't finish the chat, well, now you know.

I never went on Clubhouse again.

Memories are funny like that. Some "bad" experiences become good in the retelling. My friends and I have laughed hysterically over the retelling of my most embarrassing moment too many times to count at this point. Some "good" experiences become bad when viewed through time and the wisdom of hindsight. But have you ever thought about the idea that our reality, our reaction to everything around us, is based on memory?

Do you love dark chocolate? Are you afraid of spiders? Attracted to blondes or brunettes? Believe in heaven and hell? Play piano? Literally every part of your worldview is based on a memory you have. That's incredible when you're at a recital playing Beethoven's "Für Elise," but it's potentially limiting when you can't get over your debilitating shyness.

Wouldn't it be cool if we could pluck out any memories that negatively affect our lives without losing the lessons we learned because of the experience?

Like, imagine you woke up today and you're you—you know that's your girlfriend, or you understand that's your son, or you get that you're a PhD candidate or in school to become an RN or a single mama working at the grocery store. You know all those things about yourself, but now . . . now you have no backstories. That time your third-grade teacher told you that you had a terrible voice and shouldn't sing? Gone. The memory of your husband leaving you for another woman? Erased. Every negative story you know to be true—the things you've defined yourself by, they don't exist anymore. This concept is blowing my mind.

You are an amalgamation of your stories, but your stories, made up of memories, can only ever represent the past. If those stories didn't exist—or if at the very least your commitment to those stories didn't exist—what you'd be left with is **this present moment**. You'd have no backstory to justify why you act the way you do. The anxiety you're feeling wouldn't come with a long history that helps to support it.

Honestly, would the anxiety even be there at all if you couldn't remember having it a hundred times before?

So much of my self-work and therapy is always—always—about trying to process pain from my past. Sometimes it seems like an endless journey of healing one piece of my history after another—like trauma-based whack-a-mole. But *my God*, what if I just woke up one day and *couldn't remember* all the things I can't forget?

Who would I be then? Who would ***you*** *be then?*

Maybe I wouldn't have anxiety anymore because my anxiety is always triggered by a present moment experience *reminding me* of a past trauma. If I didn't have anxiety ever again, I imagine I'd experience a sense of freedom that I've only touched in the briefest glimpses. Those glimpses are enough to make me try to build the structure of my life around the pursuit that it's possible to completely heal from anxiety. I've learned to feel anxious over the last decade. It wasn't always part of my life despite a childhood that was filled with opportunities to develop it. If I can learn a behavior, surely I can unlearn it too. So I keep chipping away at the triggers and the pieces that hold it in place because I tell myself someday it won't have control anymore.

I was riding in an Uber once, and my driver gestured to the coffee in my hand and asked me if I was on a smoke break. When I told him I don't smoke (why would I ever want to tarnish God's perfect beverage with cigarettes?!), he told me he used to smoke three packs a day.

"I loved to have coffee with a cigarette," he told me. "But it's been fifteen years. You can't imagine how horrible the withdrawals were for me. I was like a drug addict." He thought for a minute. "I guess I *was* a drug addict."

I had to ask, "Had you tried to quit before?"

"So many times."

"And why do you think the last time actually worked?"

"You know what it was?" He laughed. "I wake up early every morning because I drive a lot of people to the airport for morning flights. Every morning I wake up at 3 or 4 a.m., and the first thing I do is have a cup of coffee and a cigarette. But one morning

I woke up and realized I didn't have any more cigarettes. I didn't even think about it; I drove to a gas station at 3 a.m. and bought cigarettes and was back home smoking one with a cup of coffee a little while later. As I sat there, I realized I hadn't actually made a decision to go to the store; I'd done it without thought. I looked at my cigarette and said, *I am not in control. This thing is controlling me.*" He scowled at the memory. "I grew up in a country that controls everything you do—there's nothing I hate more than not being in control of my life. I hated every second of quitting cigarettes, but I hated their power over me more."

Don't you love it when you interact with a spirit guide on your Uber ride?

Our memories can be a lot like that driver and his cigarettes—without paying attention and without deeper insight, they appear to be something we're in charge of, but when we peer closer, we realize they're controlling us.

As a personal development nerd, I can't help but be turned on by the idea that I could flip a switch and the negative stuff would just . . . be gone. I don't want to lose the lessons I've learned or the way my heart was softened by the experience, but if I couldn't remember the actual hard thing, I think I would feel safe enough to flourish completely. I'll keep the scars if I could only lose the memory of how I got them. Because the memory of how I got them, that has the single greatest detrimental effect on my life.

I know this because all of my anxiety stems from one single thought—something bad is going to happen. And that belief system was born inside a world where something bad *did* happen. A lot.

Even when I take adaptogens and meditate. Even when I sit through endless therapy sessions. Even when my rational mind tells my irrational nervous system that all is well and there's nothing to be afraid of. Even then, she has too many examples of times when the opposite was true. I honestly think the shock of something unexpectedly bad happening is more violent to our system than the actual occurrence.

This poor little hypervigilant, never-resting part of me, likely developed when I was a little girl, is still very much functioning as a scared child. Among all the other work I'm doing to heal that part of me, I found this fantasy idea.

What if I couldn't remember the bad stuff? What if you couldn't remember your bad stuff either? Retrograde amnesia or some pretty powerful hypnosis aside, I know this scenario isn't easily possible. But asking yourself the question certainly is.

Who would you be if you didn't have a hundred stories telling you who you are?

I think I'd be way more courageous. I'd create a lot more and in categories I've never tried before. I'd definitely know how to ride a skateboard. My childhood dreams of being just like the cool skater chicks with their colorful Vans would be made manifest. I probably wouldn't be such a prude—maybe I'd show more cleavage or wear short shorts and not hear the voices of the old church ladies of my youth gossiping about girls who dressed "that way" being no better than they ought. I'd have more fun, I'd have more friends. I wouldn't remember being hurt or disappointed by people I thought would love me forever. I wouldn't remember being lied to or betrayed. I wouldn't remember all the mistakes I've made. I wouldn't remember my shame. I'd go into every situation with my heart fully open. I'd be fluent in Spanish by now (and maybe other languages too!). I wouldn't remember how "hard" I decided it would be in the beginning, and so I'd have pursued it with curiosity and maybe even a little wonder but never as a challenge I wasn't smart enough to master. I'd be a calmer parent and not so easily frustrated by the particular brand of magic that can come from a five-year-old girl with as much will as any reigning monarch you've ever known. I'd never play small, act dumb, or fear stretching my stem out past the other poppies.

I think if I could let go of the nightmares I've lived through, I'd become the woman of my dreams. And while I know I'll never be able to erase those memories, I do believe that by identifying what I'd like to let go of, I can identify the areas my memories are still holding me hostage.

Are **YOU** the problem?

I have a superpower.

If there is someone anywhere in my vicinity in a bad mood, I will lock onto them like a homing beacon.

This superpower of mine doesn't exist so that I can seek out people with negative energy in order to Pollyanna them back into a happy state . . . even I'm not that optimistic. No, this skill exists in me—and likely every human being raised with some level of violence in their childhood home—as a safety measure. When you spend your formative years always on the alert for the smallest change in someone else's mood, it's impossible to shake that hyperawareness.

So I walk through life (and the grocery store, the airport, the gym) aware of negative or positive energy the same way a drug-sniffing dog can discern between an ounce of marijuana and a souvenir with a hidden compartment for cocaine.

I don't even need to ***see*** the bad mood. I swear to you I can feel it behind me or beside me or two tables over. It's like Eeyore's cloud, and once I'm aware of it, it's impossible for me to ignore. My friends, kids, boyfriend—they'll continue enjoying the restaurant, the concert, or the bench press at the gym while I can't drown out the sound of the couple fighting over an ex, the toxic parent verbally demolishing their teenager, or the Karen being rude to the server. Usually, this awareness will stress me out so much that

I'll start praying: for them, for me, for a hedge of protection, for a spoonful of sugar . . . literally anything I can think of to try to put some good energy into the dark situation. I am fully aware that someone else's fight, bad attitude, or grouchy mood is none of my business. I know that I should tune it out and move on, but I'm currently incapable of it. Writing this chapter for you now, I can remember the dark energy of strangers from decades ago. I'll be sure to discuss all of this at my next therapy appointment.

But before I get to the other side of this neurosis, I'd like to utilize a recent experience with it as a teachable moment. I am a writer, after all.

I was traveling with my two youngest kids. As a frequent traveler, I've got my airport arrival time down to a science. One of my other superpowers is timing an airport arrival so I can get from the parking garage to my gate *exactly* as my zone boards. This gift was honed over hundreds of flights, and it absolutely stresses most of my traveling companions the hell out. I like to think of it as both an art and a science. I'm positive that half the reason my boyfriend and I are so compatible is that he travels as much as I do and also believes in arriving at the airport with only enough time to fill up your water bottle before it's time to board.

In this instance though, I was traveling alone with kids, and the unknown variables they bring to the mix are not to be trifled with. Any parent can tell you that children will absolutely destroy an itinerary with very little effort on their part. Maybe your toddler throws up all over everyone in aisle 11 before the boarding door closes. Maybe this is the moment your five-year-old forgets that they've been potty trained for years and craps their pants while you wait in line for Jamba Juice in terminal 3.

The options are truly endless, and if you want a snowball's chance in hell of reaching your destination, you have to plan for every eventuality. Maybe you won't need three changes of clothes, a first aid kit, their birth certificate, a vial of cord blood, and the license and registration for your first car . . . *maybe* you won't need that stuff. But maybe you will, and *by God*, you better have it packed just in case! You also better get to the airport a solid three hours before you actually need to be there. Which is what I had done to find myself at the gate with well over an hour to kill before our early morning flight.

I had one kid on either side of me, but both were locked onto their iPad like a Na'vi warrior to their soulmate dragon, so they were fully occupied. Just before I could press play on the podcast I had cued up, a mother sat down on the other side of Noah with her two young daughters.

As soon as she sat down, her toddler—who was maybe eighteen months—became enamored of the fact that Noah was holding a doll. My daughter has had this baby doll (which she named Noah Jr. as soon as she was old enough to offer titles to the members of her court) since she was born. Noah Jr. is kind of a mess. Her appendages are made of hard plastic that's been scuffed from thousands of playtimes. Her torso is made of faded pink material that's been permanently stained by liquids of indeterminate origin. She's ripped and lumpy and, to no fault of her own, bald as a potato. Noah Jr. goes *everywhere* with us. She is the single most important inanimate object in my daughter's world, which makes her the single most important inanimate object in my world as well.

So as soon as the real baby started paying attention to Noah's baby, I locked in. Not because there's anything wrong with a baby taking notice but because Noah hasn't been around babies much. She's interacted almost exclusively with her three older brothers, whom she's just as likely to stab with a shiv as she is to hug them.

I was a little nervous that if this baby made a grab for Noah Jr., Noah Sr. might not react well.

My worry was for naught. This little girl's mother was so attentive to her baby (and to the baby's six-year-old sister sitting beside her) that there was nothing to fear. For fifteen minutes, I watched her mother these girls with the enthusiasm of a kindergarten teacher on her first day. You know those moms who just seem like the greatest mom?

She was that mom.

She had games and snacks and the brightest, happiest attitude with her girls; it was a wonder to behold. I was so impressed by her energy and her light . . . and then her husband walked up.

The husband—I soon overheard—had been tasked with getting the family breakfast from a nearby restaurant, and apparently, he'd committed a nuclear-level offense. The mother—someone I'd come to think of as a joyful ray of light—swiftly (and shockingly) turned vicious.

"Why do you have coffee, Brandon?" she snapped.

The man began to hand out breakfast tacos to the kids.

"What?" he asked in confusion.

"I said, *why do you have coffee*? You just got yourself a coffee and didn't get one for me?"

There are a dozen mild-mannered ways to ask a question like this, and she didn't employ any of them. She asked that question like she despised him.

My Spidey sense was tingling. I couldn't have stopped eavesdropping if my life depended on it because at that point, with that tone of voice, my imagination was running wild. I'm wondering, *What on earth did Brandon do to make her hate him like this?*

"I . . . I asked you if you wanted coffee," Brandon told her cautiously. "You said no because you don't like drip coffee. But I can go get you something if you've changed your mind."

"It's just pretty rude to get yourself coffee and not bring anything back for me," she told him while unwrapping a breakfast taco for her daughter. "If they don't have what I like, you could have—*Oh my God, why don't you ever listen?!*" she hissed at him. "I told you to get corn tortillas. We don't like flour!" She pushed the foil wrapped taco at him accusingly.

"Yeah, Daddy. We don't like flour." This was from the six-year-old, said in the same hateful tone her mother was using.

Ruh-roh, I thought.

"I asked for corn, I promise," Brandon told them both. He pointed to the sticker on the side of the taco that said "Corn."

"Well, you got it wrong," the mom told him. "Go fix it."

I tell you, this man went back and forth to that taco stand two more times. The second time he did get the corn tortillas, but his wife said they weren't warm enough. Then he went to get her an espresso drink, but that took too long according to the wife. The whole time I was a giant ball of anxiety *willing* my plane to pull into the gate so we could escape whatever toxic relationship this Dr. Jekyll / Ms. Hyde had going on with Brandon.

But then, out of nowhere, the extended family showed up. Grandparents, cousins, the whole crew—apparently this was a big family vacay. And once I got a look at the generations all assembled together, the reality of the situation became apparent.

I'm willing to bet that poor Brandon hadn't done anything to his wife to earn her ire . . . the way she was treating him was the exact way that his mother-in-law was treating her husband. Only, unlike Brandon, Pop-Pop was a shell of a human. He hovered at the edges of the family circle barely interacting but still, somehow, pissing Nana off with everything he did.

This attentive mother had been raised by an attentive mother who—I'm theorizing here—maybe decided that men are annoying and they never do anything right. The wives must control and cajole and scold them into submission, but since the men are incapable of doing it exactly how Mom would prefer it be done, they're basically worthless. It was awful to be around and even sadder to watch the little girl who was already learning this unbroken generational narrative.

Now, look, obviously I don't have the full context here.

I'm basing this entire thesis off forty minutes of observation, a minuscule window of time into this family's life. But even if I'm totally wrong about what I saw . . . we all know someone like this, right? We all have an auntie, a college roommate, a coworker, or a lifelong friend who at some point or another decided that their partner *is the problem*. It was likely a subconscious narrative made long before they'd ever actually met this partner, but still. In their mind this person is a problem to be solved, a child in need of training, and 90 percent of the time, they can do no right. This archetype shows up throughout literature and film; Shakespeare wrote a whole play about a shrew all the way back in the 1590s. But I don't see a lot of honest conversation about them. If we don't ever talk about this kind of person, then maybe you don't even know they exist. If we don't get honest about this behavior, then you might never consider that **you are the problem**.

It's easy to blame the way we're feeling (or acting!) on other people, but what if you're the one who's toxic? Maybe your partner tries their absolute hardest (or maybe they did in the beginning), but your constant dissatisfaction with every single attempt, your constant beratement at every turn, means they've given up. Or worse, maybe they've become smaller and quieter with every passing year because at least if they don't annoy you, they get a little peace. That's what was happening with Pop-Pop at the airport . . . I was observing the effects of forty years of nagging. I was looking at someone whose body was present but whose spirit had long since drawn so far inward, it was impossible to sense it there.

It's funny in a sad sort of way because if the gender situation were reversed . . . if a wife was diligently trying to get breakfast for the family and the right coffee, and we all watched her try again and again . . . if we watched her husband speak to her—and allow his sons to speak to her—the way we'd just watched happen in reverse, I think more than one stranger would have come to the woman's defense. But because it's a wife talking to her husband, everyone shrugs it off.

It's interesting how hard we fight for equality but still accept behavior as normative when it wouldn't be accepted coming from the other gender. I'm positive I could find loads of examples of this kind of thing happening in all sorts of ways, but for today's purposes, I just want to stick with one thought.

Just because you're a woman doesn't mean you aren't a bully. Just because they're your partner doesn't mean you get to treat them like crap. Being sweet and lovely to your kids isn't worth much if they watch you act nasty and hateful to anyone else . . . especially other people they care about.

I know this isn't easy to hear. I hate coming to the realization that I'm in the wrong or, even worse, that I've hurt someone else. But the discomfort of owning my role is infinitely better than continuing to inadvertently cause pain.

When my kids or my partner tell me I've done something that hurt or frustrated them, everything in me bristles. My ego shows up, ready to Hulk smash its defensive position. I have to fight my instinct to convince anyone and everyone that since I would never *intentionally* hurt them, then I definitely didn't *actually* hurt them.

It was one of the hardest lessons in the world for me to learn. My fear of getting into trouble can easily manifest into anger and defensiveness. At least with that stance—my ego tells me—I might be able to talk them around without admitting I've done anything wrong. It's taken a lot of therapy, sure, but more than anything, it's taken a lot of desensitization to receiving critical feedback: owning it, apologizing, and then working to do better. The more you practice these things, the less debilitating it is to admit when you're the one who needs to work on it.

And PS, ***we're all*** *the ones who need to work on it.*

If you have trouble controlling your anger, bitterness, or even rage—if it spills out when you don't mean for it to, I know it's hard to hear, but, friend, *you're* the problem. It doesn't make you bad or wrong or a terrible person—it just means you've got some stuff to work on. If you find the same faults in the different people around you, realize that *you* are the only common variable.

Here's the good news: if you do take full ownership of your attitude and emotions instead of blaming the way *you're* behaving on *others*, you're fully in control of changing your life for the better.

And you can.

You can change your life, your day-to-day experience, your relationship with your kids, your mental health, the balance of your hormones, the happiness you find in your relationship, the passion you experience in your job—all of it. But nothing improves without your assistance—without above all your acceptance of who you are and what you need to work on.

Who are you trying to please?

I have been talking—to anyone who would listen—since the moment I learned to form words.

As far back as my memory stretches, I remember being curious about everything around me. *How did those clouds get up there? What happened to Aunt Erma after she died? What's a scab made out of?* And so I asked and asked and asked. I assumed that any person taller than me had the answers to my questions. If I didn't have a question at a particular moment, I talked about what had happened the day before or what I saw out the car window or what my favorite parts of Christmas were.

I didn't understand then what it meant to be a verbal processor—I just knew that the world made more sense if I could talk about it. I think for some adults, this was adorably precocious, like those videos of dogs speaking human words.

I remember once lying in the bunk bed I shared with my big brother—I was relegated to the bottom bed for "safety purposes," and every younger sibling knows the disgruntlement of never getting top shelf—as I tried to wrap my mind around "forever" because in church that day, they told us that God created everything.

"So who created God?" I wanted to know.

"No one created God," Ryan told me. "He's always been here forever."

My little brain was still too young to question how a source great enough to create the solar systems—actually, all the solar systems anywhere ever—*who had been here forever and ever and always would be*, was also, weirdly, a "man" in every retelling I'd ever heard. However, I was ***not*** too young to not get totally spun out on the idea of something existing always. I circled around this for weeks and asked every adult in my life to explain it—I still don't have a good handle on this concept even thirty-five years later, but a seven-year-old asking everyone to explain infinity got attention. Maybe it was cute coming from a little girl. The golden retriever barking out *Mama*.

The thing about curiosity though is that you don't just wonder about things that other people find fascinating or adorable; you wonder about ***everything***. And maybe, after a while, this got annoying. Or at least, I remember starting to feel that I *was* annoying.

"Rachel, it's someone else's turn to answer." My second-grade teacher reminded me—again—not to raise my hand each time.

"Jabber-jabber-jabber-jabber-jabber-jabber-jabber-Jaaaaaw!" my older siblings would tease me, singsonging the theme to a cartoon about a talking shark, who, like me, also loved to chat.

"Rachel, do you ever shut up?" my father would snap.

As a mother of four children, I totally get that there are moments when your exhaustion means it's hard to listen to another lengthy explanation of someone's *Minecraft* world or you don't have any more energy to debate why, *No, you can't go skydiving. You're only nine.* And *Yes, you do have to go to sleep now. You have school tomorrow.*

But given how formative those years were in my life and how much my curiosity is central to who I am at my core, the grown-up version of me wonders just how destructive it was for that central part of me to feel scrutinized. It would have been so empowering to learn to cultivate my characteristics instead of squash them outright. But our parents can't possibly teach us emotional skills they don't have themselves. So I wasn't raised to lean into my natural interests and gifts to help them flourish . . . I was raised to be obedient. A good girl, a helper, a quiet and pleasing member of a family so catastrophically broken by the time I reached elementary school, it's a wonder my personality even registered on their lists of concerns. Or maybe it's not perplexing at all. Maybe my parents (and perhaps yours too) were very unprepared for the challenge of raising kids while they drowned under the weight of their own unresolved trauma. So rather than look inward—which no one taught them to do—they zeroed in on what they *could* control. Working long hours, providing for the family, trying to mold their children into a figment of their imagination.

A people pleaser isn't born—they're groomed into existence, often by someone who believes this is the right way to be because they were also groomed. This kind of thing goes back for generations.

People pleasers are taught very early on that they're responsible for the way other people feel. Daddy's not angry because of the unhealed damage of his own angry father; he's angry because *you didn't clean up your breakfast dish*. That's why he's yelling at you. *It's your fault.*

Your partner isn't verbally demolishing you because you finally found the courage to confront them about their behavior. Not at all. No, they're eviscerating you because *you always do this, you always want to talk when they're tired from the office, and you have no idea how hard they work, and if you didn't want them to be so angry, then why did you make them so angry?*

You learn early on to do everything you can to avoid displeasing anyone—or to at least convince yourself that it's possible. People pleasers are very easily manipulated, especially by narcissists and abusers. Unconsciously choosing a partner who reinforces the emotional manipulation we learned as a child?

We're fucking fantastic at it!

A people pleaser's job is to ensure that everybody feels happy with us. We avoid conflict at all costs. We love words of affirmation—praise makes us feel safe. We apologize constantly, even for things that aren't our fault. We don't feel comfortable telling anyone no because one of our biggest fears in life is that someone might be upset with us. This makes any kind emotional boundary feel nearly impossible to uphold. We don't want to cause any friction or make any waves so we'll agree and go along with the plan, even if it's not what we want to be doing. What should we eat for dinner? Oh, I don't know, *what do you want?*

For the part of me still trapped in the psychology of my childhood, there's no difference in who might be upset with me or why they're angry. The truck in the grocery store parking lot who zoomed around me in a huff because I was too slow feels the same as a stranger on social media telling me they hate me because I got divorced, feels the same as my son's teacher calling to inform me that he was misbehaving at school today. Rationally, as I sit here typing this, I know this doesn't make any sense. My mind is clear, and my heart is full, and I don't currently have anxiety in my body . . . so right now, ever getting so upset about stupid (and often made-up) scenarios seems impossible. I wonder sometimes about those of you who aren't people pleasers—my God, *what is that like?!* Do you just—I don't know—*live?* Can you make it through hours (or days?!) without wondering what other people think of you?

For those of us who were reared to avoid being "bad" at all costs, it's incredibly difficult to stop looking for others to validate our goodness. And have you ever thought about the fact that "good" and "bad" are in the eye of the beholder? My mom's mom, we call her Mema, she'd go apoplectic if she ever heard you say "gosh." In her opinion, *the Lord knows what's in your heart; he knows you don't really mean gosh . . . you mean to take his name in vain, but you're being sneaky*. That was grounds to go cut your own switch of the willow tree out front.

By contrast, some of the most inspiring and spiritual people I've known in my life love to smoke weed, enjoy a great bottle of wine, and throw out their favorite cuss words like confetti. Mema would not approve. But can you see how good and bad are the discernment of whoever's doing the judging?

If you're loud and dramatic but your parents prefer quiet and demur, you'll adjust your true nature to accommodate them. If you're a wild child who pushes boundaries and refuses to back down to anyone, but the only way your new stepmom will accept you is through perfect obedience, you will become something other than you are. If you want to move cross-country to become a choreographer, but your family's mantra is doctor/lawyer/CPA, the people pleaser in you will go to great lengths to ensure that you don't upset anybody by being yourself.

Oh, it's such a hard cycle to break! But it really is possible to escape your people pleasing and maybe not in as dramatic a fashion as you've imagined. Contrary to what your anxious mind would have you believe, the antidote to your people pleasing isn't to become a selfish bastard who alienates everyone they love. It doesn't have to be a wholesale deconstruction of your entire life—though that can be fun too if you've got the time.

You stop being a people pleaser when you start ***pleasing yourself***.

No, not in a Divinyls kind of way—though, again, that can be fun too if you've got the time. The antidote to people pleasing, beyond perhaps the therapy to figure out its origins in your life, is to put your energy into figuring out what you actually like and enjoy. Why? Because people pleasers have rarely even considered it! We're so busy trying to do what everyone else wants or needs, it doesn't occur to us that we might also want some things or need some stuff or prefer the thermostat at seventy-two instead of sixty-four.

I like movies about fantasy worlds where creatures have hard-to-pronounce names and at least one wizard shows up. I like to leave the windows open rather than have the air conditioner on. I like wind chimes and bird feeders. **I love fresh dill.** I love dill on roast potatoes with butter and garlic. I love dill aggressively taking up space in a tartar sauce. I love when it sneaks its way into a salad or rides piggyback on roast salmon. My ex hated dill—no shade to him; I'm sure lots of people do—but I never cooked with it, not in eighteen years. When I got divorced? It was dill-a-palooza! I put it on everything!

I cannot explain how happy it made me to do simple things like grocery shop or choose a movie to watch when the only person I was trying to please was myself. It was simple. It was small, insignificant choices. It was revolutionary.

It took being by myself to understand that I was allowed to advocate for myself. I hope it isn't the same for you. You can begin to make decisions today, one choice at a time, that will teach you to feel safe saying what you really want and think and need. It starts with little things like what you'd really like to have for dinner, or asking for a break when you need one, or saying no thank you to running the church rummage sale this year. It grows into a foundation that helps you build those emotional boundaries you so desperately need.

Why do you believe what you believe?

When I was thirty-eight years old, for the second time *ever* in my adult life, I had a first kiss.

No, I'm not some mole person who's been trapped in an underground bunker. No, I have not been living off the grid out in the middle of nowhere. *shutters in bougie* No, I did not just leave a convent—though *damn*, I do often dream of a life where I live alone with all my girlfriends wearing long flowy dresses and no boys are allowed.

My story is this: I was eighteen years old when I met the man who would become my ex-husband. When I met him, I was bright eyed and bushy tailed . . . and also a pastor's daughter, which is to say: a *big ole* virgin who had never done anything with anyone, ever. Unless, wait—do you count spin the bottle in sixth grade when you were hoping to land on Michael Foster but landed on Jack Stevenson instead?

No?

You don't count that?

OK, then I stand by my original statement. When I met my ex-husband, I had the sexual experience of a sea slug.

We were together for eighteen years. That's the same amount of time it takes to raise someone into adulthood—it turns out, that someone was me. The "eighteen years" bit is important though: it included the last of my teen years, all of my twenties, and most of my thirties too. At the end of that relationship, while I was sexually experienced in terms of, shall we say, miles logged, I wasn't necessarily experienced in terms of "new terrain."

So back to that second first kiss . . .

A year or so postdivorce and deeply inside of a global pandemic, I found myself . . . bored? I have the most hilarious, fun, and extremely time-consuming *four* children *and* a robust career I'm deeply passionate about, so, no, I won't say bored. I also won't say lonely because the level of fun I had with my friends inside of a COVID bubble together is illegal in at least two states.

So not lonely either, but I was craving . . . adventure.

Truthfully, if I had been able to travel the world, you and I would not be having this conversation. But since travel wasn't an option for any of us at that point, the "adventure" that I chose to have instead was dating.

I went with *dating* . . . for the first time ever . . . in my adult life. And, y'all, I had ***no*** idea how to go about it.

Like, how much had dating changed in the nearly twenty years since I'd met exactly one man and married him as fast as I could? How on earth was I supposed to connect with someone during a pandemic? Did I even want to meet someone?? And if I did meet them, were we supposed to talk? Did people still call it "talking"?

I was so confused.

And those were just the parts of *dating* that confused me. That was actually the least stressful bit. The most stressful bit? Sex.

What do you call it when you've had a lot of sex but only with one partner? I'm not going to feign humility here; I thought of myself as a bit of a sexual expert. A sexpert, if you will.

But then, suddenly, I was faced with the harsh reality that

maybe I was only skilled *with one person*. Perhaps what made me great in the sack wasn't skill so much as tenure. And now I was supposed to try with someone new?

That thought only led to another, more terrifying one that sounded something like this in my head: *OH, HOLY CRAP BALLS! I'M GOING TO SEE A NEW PENIS!* At that point, I only had experience with the one penis I knew. Now I had to navigate the knowledge of a whole new landscape?! ***And*** not all penises are the same, er, dimensions, right? Because I only knew the one shape I was familiar with. What if the new penis looked different than what I was expecting? I don't have a very good poker face; what if I showed some kind of visible reaction when I saw a new penis? What if I flinched? *Oh my God*, what if I scarred some poor man for life because my reaction seemed negative when, really, it's just surprise?

I was *stressed out*. I had so many questions and worries and irrational fears. I definitely wasn't ready to be intimate again, but surely that would happen at some point, and how would it work? Like, what do I say after I have sex for the first time? Is it like yoga? *The divine light in me bows to the divine light in you. Namaste.*

The level of awkward I was toting into this new endeavor cannot be properly quantified. Which brings me back around to where this started. That kiss.

There was this man—a *gorgeous* man with perfect hair and beautiful eyes, but I'm not going to tell you about him. I *am* going to tell you about this kiss. More specifically, the moment when I realized I was about to be kissed, and my internal litany started speaking in tongues like a Pentecostal on Palm Sunday.

My brain started screaming, and my heart—I swear to God, my heart felt like it was going to explode. And suddenly we were kissing, and it's so wonderful and perfect and romantic that what *was a heart attack* now felt like my entire nervous system was shutting down.

Was I wheezing? Maybe.

Was I sweating through my clothes? Most definitely.

And *what*, what did I—successful, highly accomplished, wildly confident, badass that I am—what did I do when this beautiful man started kissing me?

I froze. I froze like an animal about to be hit by a car.

My lips stopped moving.

My inner monologue was still going rapid-fire, and only now could I make out the words: *How do I move my lips? Oh Lord, wait, how does kissing work? Do I use tongue?*

Forget tongue, at that point I started worrying about things that don't even happen in kissing, but I was freaking out so badly, I couldn't think straight! *Do I use teeth? Do I need the blood of a spring chicken? When does the Pythagorean theorem come into play?*

And honestly, y'all, I wish—*I freaking wish*—I could tell you it stopped there. But even worse than forgetting how to work my lips was what I did with my arms. I couldn't remember where my hands should go, so I just sort of held them out to the sides . . . in the air, you guys! Like a dolphin performing a trick or the Human Torch summoning fire. It was . . . it was not even the worst of it.

The worst of it was when I started to narrate. Audibly.

Unfortunately, yes, I, Rachel, in a panicked state with numb lips and exploding heart and arms floating at ten and two, did *in fact* start to audibly narrate what was happening.

Imagine something like, "Oh my gosh you're kissing me and that feels nice and my lips aren't moving and my mouth is so dry—is your mouth dry? where do my teeth go?—and . . ."

Can you—*can you even imagine?*

It was embarrassing and awkward and mortifying and also . . . fucking spectacular.

Yes, it was fucking spectacular.

Turns out, even the most disjointed first kiss is still magic, especially when you've waited so long to experience it. Turns out, at thirty-eight, it's unbelievably delicious to be so nervous about someone's lips against yours that you start hyperventilating. Turns out that even if you don't know what you're doing, you can still enjoy every second of it.

After that man left my front porch and drove away into the night, I lay on my bed for hours—literally hours—rubbing my fingers back and forth across lips that were still tingling. Yes, it feels a little embarrassing to admit that I acted like a teenager in a '90s rom-com, but since I never expected to feel like that again, I'm going to go ahead and cherish the memory right here on this page.

That night stacks up with so many other memories in the last five years that I never believed I'd experience. There are beautiful memories and hard soul-crushing moments and wonder and serendipity that can only be divine. I have changed and grown and been stretched beyond what I thought I could bear. In the wake of all these things, what I've discovered is that so many of my beliefs, so many of my capital-*T* truths have fallen one after another like dominoes. In the absence of all I thought I knew were gaping holes. "I've been 'fraid of changing, 'cause I've built my life around you . . ." Now you know why I cry so hard at Stevie Nicks concerts.

The years following my divorce were filled almost entirely with questions—not an easy space to exist in for someone who likes to be in control. But I now see that sitting in the discomfort of *not knowing* was crucial. In many ways, the searching I did during that time allowed me to find, if not truth, then at least an acceptance that made me infinitely stronger than I was before.

Trees are like that too. It's not calm, easy springtime that allows them to stand the test of time—it's the violent gales that tear at them throughout the winter. The oppositional force of the wind forces them to grow a foundation strong enough to hold them upright. The roots made up of questions—those were the impetus for this book.

One of the biggest questions of the bunch, the greatest one for me to grapple with, was why I believe what I do. And how had the blind acceptance of those beliefs potentially hurt me as a result?

Why do I believe what I believe?

Why do you?

About anything.

About everything.

But most especially, why do I (or you) still fall into traps wrapped in beliefs about who we're "supposed" to be? Why do we believe what we do about our worth, our capabilities, our place in this world, or the way we're "supposed" to show up? Why do we believe what we do about sex, success, or shame? Why do we believe what we do about others or ourselves?

Why did I spend most of my childhood and early adult life believing that, even after divorce, even in my late thirties, having sex outside of marriage was deeply sinful and confirmation that I was a whore? And why is it that I never really saw that disgusting patriarchal narrative for what it was? I didn't, in fact, really think about how antiquated this notion is until I was a grown-up single woman who realized that while I *would* like to have sex again someday, there was a zero percent chance I'd get married again in order to have it.

Stacy Schiff has a line I love so much that I keep it in the notes app on my phone: "We all subscribe to preposterous beliefs," she writes. "We just don't know yet which ones they are." It's a moment in her book *Witches*, and she's referring to Salem in 1692 and to people who used religious ideology to oppress women.

Thank goodness that doesn't still happen today . . . oh, wait.

There are innumerable examples of harmful paradigms that each and every one of us exist inside of . . . and those paradigms morph and change with every iteration, culture, and kind of human in existence. Most of us are so busy trying to emotionally keep our heads above water that the last thing we're questioning is why we're drowning in those feelings in the first place. Or maybe we do dig in and figure out "what's wrong," but we really only ever found the first layer . . . there was a whole onion of unpeeling left to do. My layers surrounding just this **one** topic included: sex, intimacy, body image, faith, good girl syndrome, anxiety, and *a lot* of questions and insecurity about the right length my pubic hair should be.

And under each of those layers? You guessed it! More freaking layers!! It's a lot of onion to deal with, and why would you want to? Going through the onion's layers almost always makes you cry. But in the recipe of your life, it'll stay pretty bland if you don't.

Perhaps you begin to peel away and discover that your beliefs feel central and aligned with the person you are today. How wonderful.

What's more common though is that when we begin to work through our layers, we often find someone else's creation. These aren't our core values but the ideologies of our parents, the religion we were born into, our culture, or even ancestral behaviors we never signed up for. We might discover that we've been unconsciously living out someone else's viewpoints simply because we never questioned them.

Want an easy way to see if that's what you've been doing? Tune into the negative voice that plays on repeat in the back of your mind. I'm not talking about your intuition (which is always kind and supportive); I mean the hurtful self-talk that everybody I know has. Think about that voice, think about the things it says to you—especially the criticism you've heard from it one thousand times before. You're ugly, you're fat, you're dumb, you'll never make it . . . you know the one. *That* voice.

Is that voice a man or a woman? Is it young or old? If you had to give that voice a name and a hairstyle and a favorite outfit, what would it be? What would that voice look like if they were a real person?

Here's what never ceases to amaze me: in all the years of giving people that prompt, I've never—not even one time—had somebody describe themselves.

It's never ***their*** voice saying hateful things. It's some creation of their imagination that, at least in my case, bears a shocking resemblance to the authority figure I was most afraid of as a child. My own personal psychology notwithstanding, let's circle back around to you and all the beliefs you have. The voice of judgment that tries to rule your mind? It's not yours.

If it's not your voice, why do you allow it to keep talking?

What are you afraid to admit?

I have written so many things about pregnancy and motherhood because, honestly, it's a go-to when your readership is primarily women.

Motherhood is one of the most unifying topics I know of because no matter how different we all are or how differently we approach it, we're way more alike as moms than different. I've written about it a ton for those reasons but also because writing is my way to process hard things and motherhood is really, really hard sometimes.

My ability to grow three of my four children inside of my body and then push them safely out into the world is one of the greatest, coolest things I've ever been a part of. But also, in some ways, labor was traumatic.

It was scary and hard. It literally ripped me open.

Then after being ripped open and sewn back together while bleeding from both my nether regions *and my nipples* (WTF?!), I had to care for another—extremely delicate—human being. It was the craziest, most brutal experience I've ever gone through . . . and I was not warned about it by any woman I knew. Ever.

How is that possible? How is it possible that women endure

this incredible—and, yes, sometimes awful—thing, but nobody tells the full truth?

Because a good mom isn't supposed to complain.

One of my girlfriend's babies got stuck in her birth canal, and no matter how hard she pushed, her baby girl wouldn't budge. The baby's heart rate began to plummet, making an already terrifying situation life or death. The forceps they had to use to get the baby out quickly gave her mama a fourth-degree tear.

If you're not familiar with that term, I'm sorry to tell you that it's when you rip open from your vagina all the way to your anus. Just to reiterate: a doctor slid giant metal tongs inside her vagina, used them to grasp her baby's head like a plush from the claw machine, and forcibly removed her baby back out of her vagina. And they did all of this with such force that it ripped my friend open like a piñata.

When she went into labor, she had a hole for her vagina and a hole for her butt—but in that moment, it all became one giant hole.

No, seriously, WTF?!

Her memory of the entire experience is horrific. And the physical effects of those tears and scars and stitches will be with her for the rest of her life. But she doesn't really talk about it because a good mama isn't supposed to complain.

Another friend of mine had a panic attack during her C-section because the anesthesia made her go completely numb from the neck down. She was positive she was suffocating because she could no longer feel her lungs breathe in and out. But she doesn't really talk about it. A good mama isn't supposed to complain.

Y'all, those are just a few of my mom horror stories, *and that's just about labor and delivery*. If I got into the hardships of actually raising those babies once you get them back home, we'd be here all month! And, look, for every one of these hard stories, of course there are five more that are positive and beautiful, but I am so sick of all the things we're taught to hide away for fear that we will be judged if we mention them. Including, and especially, the truths that would help *so many people* if they knew that they aren't alone when they struggle. It would also be great if we had a little more information before we blindly walk into situations where our labia is about to be stretched out.

We should be able to talk about the hard parts of our lives without the implication that we're ungrateful.

So I will.

Being a mama is literally the greatest gift in my whole life. I feel lucky just to *know* my kids. The fact that I also get to be their mom? *How on earth did I get this privilege?*

But let's be real . . . it's forty-one-year-old Rachel writing this book.

Twenty-four-year-old Rachel is the one who got pregnant for the first time, and she had no idea what to expect.

In my forties, I'm calmer and more centered. At this age, I've raised four children of my own over the last seventeen years as well as loved four little girls in foster care. At this age I've done therapy and learned to manage my hormones, and I am *so, so, so* much more graceful with myself and others. It's easy for me to sit here *now* and tell you that I'm blessed and happy and feeling great as a mom because I've had the time to figure it out. But back in the day? I was a mess, life was a mess, and *maybe* that would have been fine if I'd had some kind of warning.

But *what the hell, man?* Nobody warned me!

How about some preparation? How about you toss a new parent a bone? Basically, every single person I knew back then who had a child but didn't try to help prepare me is a jerk. You know what those fools told me? Things like "I never knew I could love something so much!" or "Make sure you get these baby moccasins; they're the only ones that stay on."

Baby shoes? That's your advice?!

Remember that scene in *Mulan* (which is my favorite Disney movie, by the way) where Mushu—voiced to perfection by Eddie Murphy—is like, "DISHONOR! Dishonor on *you*, dishonor on your family, dishonor on your *cow* . . ." That's me, I'm Mushu, and every friend who knew how hard it was going to be but didn't try to prepare me is the cow.

PS: The "cow" is actually a horse in the movie; that has nothing to do with this conversation, but it's important to me that my fellow Disney lovers know *that I know* that I'm part of their world.

PPS: Yes, that was **two** Disney references in a row. #Mom

Nobody said anything to prepare me, I'm guessing because nobody said anything to prepare *them*, and also once someone is due to have a baby, what are you gonna say?

Nothing.

You're going to keep your mouth shut because you don't want to freak them out. Then you'll make sure to show up after all hell breaks loose with a box of diapers and a casserole that freezes beautifully and help that new parent the best you can.

But, y'all, I didn't need a casserole; I needed a plan. But I didn't know what I didn't know, so I thought that my only prep work was to wash all the onesies in that special newborn detergent.

I will never forget my first labor. Or the feeling of the doctor placing my son Jackson on my chest. I've never had such a visceral moment of recognition—I never believed past lives might be real until we looked at each other. *Hello, little one. I know you.*

I loved him fiercely. From that first day to this one—he's almost eighteen now—I have loved that little baby with every particle of my being. And if loving your kids was all that mattered, I wouldn't have written all these books about everything that came after.

The love you feel for your children will never be enough to ignore your own emotional distress no matter how strong your bond is. My body changed in so many ways during and after pregnancy: weight gain, leaky boobs, cracked nipples, stretch marks. My emotions were all over the place after Jackson was born, and the lack of sleep only compounded it. I genuinely felt like I was losing my mind.

But the worst—the absolute worst—part was that I didn't really like being a mom. I loved my baby, but I didn't love being a mom.

There was no way I could have anticipated feeling that because I'd never heard any other mom talk about it—why would they? The stories I heard were about how great it all was. So when it didn't feel great to me?

I felt like the worst person alive.

I'm writing about this now because I want to talk to you about the relationship between motherhood and mental health. That time period as a new mom was a catalyst for some really negative emotions in me. But before I go there, I want to make sure I finish up this conversation for the mamas in case you read what I wrote above and think, "Oh my gosh, that's me. I hate being a mom sometimes, and I don't want to say it aloud, and I feel like an asshole!"

OK, here's some mom truth from me that will hopefully make you feel better about you:

1. You're not an asshole. You're a human being, and although every book and movie wants us to believe otherwise, not every mom feels like she's a natural. Some of us have to work at it. **I'm one of those moms who had to work at it.** I had to *work* to

learn how to be a mom in the way that felt good for me and my babies. Serena Williams had to *learn* how to play tennis . . . and she's the greatest tennis player that ever was! Just because motherhood didn't come naturally to you *yet* doesn't mean it won't feel natural at some point.

2. I don't like babies. *Did you just gasp and clutch your pearls?* That's cool. I know it's not something moms are supposed to say, but that's why I'm saying it. But let me elaborate: I don't like being a mom to babies—or toddlers either, for that matter. I've done it eight times—lest you forget—and every time it was incredibly stressful to me. The sweet snuggles and fun times wearing the baby in a wrap on my chest were not enough to make up for diapers and sleep training and teething. I really didn't like it, and if you've got a baby and you're feeling the same, let me tell you something incredible: it's only a season. When my oldest was a toddler and my youngest was a baby, I didn't realize it was a season. I just thought I was a terrible person who *should* love my life but didn't. But then my oldest got older, and like magic, I really began to love being a mom, and I had one of the greatest realizations of my life. I don't like being a mom to babies, but I was literally *made to be a mom* to kids who are out of toddler years. So if you have little people and you're struggling this season, please hear me: it gets better! My two oldest are teenagers now, and I actually can't believe how much fun we have and how cool it is to watch them become adults. If the season of parenting you're in feels impossible, give yourself (and your kid) the benefit of the doubt. Trust that it will get better. Until it does, triple down (quadruple down!) on taking care of **yourself** in order to take care of them.
3. You need a "messy mom" for a friend. OK, here's what you're gonna do. The next time you're at mommy-and-me yoga or

preschool pickup, I want you to peep out the other parents. You see that group of moms with pulled-together outfits and fresh blowouts? Ignore them. Keep looking. OK, see that mom who just rolled in late, and you're not sure she showered today, and she's wearing a Led Zeppelin T-shirt? Yeah, the one who watches her kid eat sand and doesn't stop him? Instead she's like, "A cat has probably peed in there and now it's in your mouth, Juaquin. Are you sure you're down with that?" **THAT'S who you need.** You need some messy moms. You need some come-over-in-your-sweatpants moms. You need some too-much-coffee-drinking, laugh-until-you-bust-your-episiotomy-stitches, there-for-you-without-pressure-or-expectations moms! You need moms in your life who you can call and say, "My kids are the literal worst!" and they won't judge you because they'll be like, *"No way, your kids can't be the worst because **MY** kids are the worst!"* Then you don't feel like such a monster because *you* know you love your kids, and so does she. You're doing your very best, but this is hard. This is hard—you need some realness in your corner of the sandbox.

Now let's talk about our mental health and how it's deeply entwined with our hormones. Motherhood, no matter how you come about it, can whack both of those things the hell out. A few years ago, I started to experience emotional mood swings that were so intense and debilitating, I genuinely thought I was experiencing a mental health crisis. I have a significant mental illness in my family tree and worried that getting older meant I was finally experiencing the symptoms.

I would swing wildly between sadness and rage. I'd be fine one moment and then have a debilitating anxiety attack the next. The next day I'd be so depressed, I couldn't leave my bed. The next

I'd experience a violent internal rage. On days I felt OK, my mind was cloudy, and my ability to focus (a cornerstone of who I know myself to be) was MIA. I was totally out of control, and since I thought it was mental, I went to see a neurologist to have every panel and test run I could get my hands on. It was during that process (which required a lot of bloodwork) that I found out I had an extreme hormone imbalance. My estrogen levels were through the roof, with my progesterone unable to keep up. While on the phone with the doctor to get the results, he asked me to google estrogen dominance and see if any of the symptoms resonated. I opened up my search screen, and as soon as the results popped up, I started bawling.

I had every single one of the symptoms.

I was emotionally unstable. I was struggling mentally. And it was 100 percent related to my hormones. I had never really learned much about my hormones—at that point, I didn't even know how my cycle worked—so I had no idea hormones could so drastically affect our health.

I met with a naturopath doctor and started a handful of natural supplements that, along with a change in my diet, drastically improved my life. When I realized what my problem actually was and subsequently how easy it was to fix, I became a little obsessive. I read every book I could get my hands on about women's bodies, women's health, menstruation, perimenopause, menopause—I wanted all of the information!

Because here's the thing: nobody ever told me this stuff . . . in fact, I'm thinking there's a pretty strong chance that nobody ever told you this stuff either. A few shocking facts for today's purposes? Did you know that fluctuating hormones related to ovulation can actually trigger existing mental health issues, causing a psychotic break or a schizophrenic episode? Or did you know that the rate of suicide ideation and attempts increase drastically in the few days before a person's period begins?

Yeah, me neither!

Imagine if even one time in a health class, instead of teaching us about male "nighttime emissions," we learned that our mental health would be affected in real and serious ways—every month! Imagine if *any doctor ever* told us, "Hey, suicidal ideology increases during these days, so it's imperative that you track your cycle and tell me if you ever feel like your mental health is being affected by it."

Friends, that's just how our psychological health is affected by a typical, fluctuating cycle when our hormones aren't in balance. What do you think might happen to our bodies when we go through pregnancy, labor, and delivery . . . and then throw sleep deprivation into the mix? Right. It's a lot. There's so much going on, and, yes, it's beautiful and wonderful. It can also be, for some women, incredibly destructive to our mental and emotional equilibrium.

Whether you're really struggling or just having a hard time, there are things we can do and *there is help you can get*. From calling in reinforcements so you can get some much-needed sleep all the way up to the proper medical care for your mental health—there is help. But if we continue to suffer in silence, if we continue to pretend that everything is fine because "a good mom isn't supposed to complain," we keep perpetuating a stigma around asking for help.

What are the things you're afraid to admit about how you're struggling? I promise you—*promise you*—whatever it is, you are not alone; there is help, and it can get better.

What's your preferred form of self-sabotage?

I spent most of my early twenties in a state of suffering.

I wasn't aware of any *emotional* struggle at the time. Truth be told, I was so detached from my feelings back then that I don't think I could have authentically admitted them even to myself.

My suffering was entirely physical.

My back hurt constantly, and I couldn't even touch my shins let alone my toes. I had extreme inflammation from all the processed junk food I was eating. Of course, at the time I didn't know the word *inflammation* or understand how processed food affected my body. I had headaches all of the time because I never, ever drank water, and I took ibuprofen constantly because that's the only way I knew of to counteract how crappy I felt. I had horrible insomnia from undiagnosed PTSD and way too much caffeine and sugar. I got winded walking up the stairs to my second-floor condo from all those "only when I drink" cigarettes.

Exercise wasn't even on my radar. Oh, sure, I'd get a new gym membership in January because all the marketing told me to, but come June, when I'd only gone seven times, I'd cancel it in a shame-faced phone call to the gym.

I feel like I'm describing a completely different person—I guess that's exactly what I'm doing because even as I'm writing it all out for you now, those choices feel totally alien to me. My late teens and twenties were filled with many harmful limiting beliefs, but the most powerful one was this: I thought everyone lived that way.

It never occurred to me that there was any other way to be because everyone I knew was in the exact same place.

Have you ever experienced that in your friend group or your family or your school? When everyone around you is making the same choices, you start to believe *those are the only choices*. If everyone around you is unhealthy, unhealthy becomes the standard. Suffering becomes the norm.

And those were the more common ways I suffered. There are also loads of uncomfortable or embarrassing things nobody talks about, right? Wearing a dress to my cousin's wedding and not being able to walk right at the reception because my thighs had rubbed each other raw. Getting stretch marks all across my butt, thighs, stomach, and arms long before I ever got them from pregnancy. Acne, brain fog, severe PMS. Extreme constipation—yeah, I'm going there—because my nutrition was abysmal.

Maybe that's too much for me to say, maybe you don't want to hear about things like that. But I bet, right now, someone reading this is living the same kind of life I was living—or possibly even worse—and they think it's normal. They think it's the most they can hope for out of their life and that acceptance fuels a string of self-sabotage that's rarely interrupted. Because make no mistake, every time I tried a fad diet or wasted money on that New Year's gym membership, I thought I was making a change. I was really only setting myself up for the same kind of disappointment I'd experienced many times before. Doing the work to get "healthy" without doing the work on your heart and spirit? At best, you improve the way you look—which absolutely can have a positive effect on the way you feel—but without healing the root cause of your *dis-ease*, you're bound to repeat it.

Self-sabotage, whether conscious or not, is when you do (or don't do) something that creates more distance between where you are and where you want to be. It can come in the form of procrastination, self-medicating with drugs or alcohol, constantly changing your plans so that you never fully commit to anything, destroying relationships—the list can go on and on. For me, self-sabotage has always come back to food. I'm guessing that's because there is so much emotion and history wrapped up for me in food. It's been my friend, my comfort, and an easily accessible source of joy my whole life. Unfortunately, it's also been a way to punish myself, a way to deprive myself, and an instant trigger that I've "failed again" by eating something "bad." I had so many negative stories around my relationship with food, and they were reaffirmed every time I destroyed my progress and momentum with self-sabotage. Unfortunately I never saw the sabotage for what it was . . . I just thought I wasn't strong enough mentally to withstand temptation or hadn't found the right diet yet.

But I didn't spend a decade carrying around fifty extra pounds of fat on my frame because I hadn't tried Atkins yet—I spent a decade fifty pounds overweight because I hadn't found therapy yet. I was fifty pounds overweight not because I didn't know about exercise but because I didn't know that *consistent effort* mattered more than initial excitement and as long as you stand back up and go again, you're still in the race, no matter how many times you fall. I wasn't self-sabotaging because I hadn't found the right shake or bought the perfect pedometer. I lacked vitality and hovered at lower emotional states because I hadn't dealt with all the baggage and trauma that made me choose unhealthy coping mechanisms in the first place. When I finally learned how to heal my spirit from past pain, I began to want to heal my body in the present too.

That was one of the key elements I wanted to teach about when I was able to plan personal development conferences over a decade later. Women would fly in from all over the country to spend a few days working on themselves and meeting other people who were interested in doing the same. When we first built the RISE conference, we chose the name because it's a verb. *To rise* requires active participation on your part. During each of those weekends, I was always astounded at how authentically the participants showed up. There is fierce energy in a group of people willing to reveal their scars. Far from being a sign of weakness, they unified our community: warriors, each and every one.

One of the most profound moments of the whole conference came during an activity we did during every event.

We would hand out a list of statements to the audience and ask them to anonymously check a box next to all that applied to them.

The prompts are raw and real and sometimes painful:

I have been physically abused.

I abuse alcohol as a way to cope.

I have lost a child.

I have been raped.

The intention is to ask women to be honest with themselves (sometimes for the first time) about how much pain and trauma they carry around with them. Most of us will endure something extremely difficult in our life, but rarely are we given the time and space we need to heal. Instead we're required to keep going because we have so many people counting on us to do just that. At the very least, it's important for us to understand how much we carry and how that kind of baggage affects us physically, emotionally, and spiritually.

So I ask them to anonymously fill out a questionnaire about their life. Then I ask them to fold it up and hand it to the woman next to them. That's when all the air comes out of the room . . . nobody wants the total stranger beside them to learn about their hardest moments in life. But then I ask them to pass the paper again. And again. And again. Until nobody knows where their own answers sit in the crowd, and since nobody put their name on the paper, it's impossible to know who wrote what.

In a world of feeling unseen and unknown, just the awareness that someone—anyone—knows your story is enough to make most people feel less alone.

Then comes the *really* powerful part.

Up on stage, I read each line of the questionnaire, and I ask the audience to stand up if the paper they're holding has that box checked.

We call it "Stand Up for Your Sister."

The idea being that it feels easier to help someone else carry *their baggage* than it is to unpack our own. It also equalizes the room because you realize that every single one of us has gone through hard things. It wasn't until our second year of conference at a small theater in a suburb of LA that I added a line about body image.

"I hate the way I look." I stood onstage, reading off the wrinkled paper in my hand.

Most of the room stood up.

If I had to guess, I'd estimate only fifty women remained seated in a room of eight hundred. Roughly 750 people responded in the affirmative when asked if they hated the way they looked. Not *disliked* the way they look. Not wished they could change something. Hate.

I was visibly taken aback. My eyes filled with tears, and the emcee had to finish reading the list for me because she could tell I was struggling.

I'd redone the prompts myself just the week before. At the last minute, I realized we didn't have anything on the list about self-love and our relationships with our bodies. When I added that statement to the list, I had no idea how much it would resonate.

Sure, almost every woman on the planet can tell you at least one thing they'd adjust about their appearance. But to admit that you *hate yourself*? That tells me that you must spend the majority of your time in some sort of self-loathing, even if you do it subconsciously.

This is heartbreaking. It's also not your fault.

Me and all those women who stood up and maybe you too . . . most of us were *taught* to hate ourselves. We're fixated on how we appear to the rest of the world because we believe acceptance and approval from others will make us worthy. So we live inside a constant battle with ourselves that we can never, ever win. The standard of beauty is forever shifting further and further out of reach **and the game is rigged**. But nobody tells you that, because if you knew it's all BS, they couldn't keep selling you things you don't need. The diet industry is worth ninety billion for a reason.

You think you can hate yourself to healthy?

Maybe you've never thought about it in those terms, but I bet on some level, most people—women especially—make choices based on that very belief. Like, if you just focus enough on your flaws, it will motivate you to get better, right?

Wrong.

It never works that way.

Wait, you say, *all those alpha fitness bros talk about boot camps and how the drill sergeant roaring at them was the exact humiliation they needed to make change. It must work!*

Let's be clear: you *can* hate yourself to **thin**.

You can hate yourself to toned. You can even hate yourself to the most coveted, model-gorgeous physique with a million followers and a brand deal for tummy tea—but you will *never* hate yourself healthy.

Real health is mind, body, and spirit. It's impossible for any one of those three to flourish in disdain.

The diet industry tells us if only you can *look* a certain way, you will *feel* a certain way, but it's actually the opposite. If you're unhappy on the *inside*, it doesn't matter what the *outside* looks like. But interestingly enough, if you are happy on the inside—your outside begins to change along with your inner vibration.

I started this chapter by asking you your favorite form of self-sabotage. Maybe you thought that was an odd turn of phrase . . . nobody actually has a "favorite" version of hurting themselves, do they?

Sit with it a moment and be honest . . . I bet you do.

I do. I *still do*, and I've been working on mine for decades.

That's because self-sabotage ***always aligns*** with self-belief.

We don't do things based on who we want to be or who we think we *should be* but always, *always* based on who we believe we are on a subconscious level.

There are things you can do to hack the system: create new routines, practice repetition, rehearse behaviors until it starts to rewire your identity at an elemental level. All of those are incredible tools. But there's one single thing you can do to disrupt the existing patterns of self-sabotage and lay the groundwork for fundamental change: learn to love yourself.

Please don't roll your eyes or dismiss this as fluffy sentiment. *Loving yourself* is the key. It's the key to a better life, it's the key to more success, to feeling good and, yes, looking good too. It's everything. But it's not something they can package and sell in a pill or a potion, so you won't hear it talked about often as a solution to health.

Think about the person you love most in the world: your bestie, your mama, your partner, your child, your dog. Would you knowingly make choices that keep them in physical pain like you do with yourself? Would you want them self-medicating the way you do? Would you feed them nutrition you know is terrible for them, then eviscerate them verbally for eating the exact thing you told them to? Would you constantly list out their flaws every time you saw them? Would you remind them of their past failures again and again and then encourage them to do the exact thing that pushed them off course last time? Would you follow around behind them spewing hate talk the way your internal monologue does about yourself?

Of course you wouldn't, because you love them truly and completely. You want them to experience pleasure and joy. You want them to feel good and happy and safe.

Have you ever thought about loving yourself that way?

If your upbringing was anything like mine, it never occurred to you. Growing up, nobody ever taught me to love myself . . . nobody ever even talked about it. Parents can't teach us knowledge they never acquired. Children can't tell the difference between a healthy coping mechanism and a bad one. I bet if you look at many of your self-sabotage techniques, they will mirror behavior you saw as an example growing up.

I'm willing to bet that most of those women who stood up at the RISE conference that day are unhappy with their health, which makes them unhappy with their appearance. They hate the feeling of inflammation in their joints that reminds them that they're abusing themselves with food. They hate the red cheeks that tell them they're consuming too much alcohol. They hate the weak arms that remind them they're not physically strong. They hate the discolored skin that reminds them their nutrition is abysmal. They hate the wrinkles around their lips that scream to the world they're still smoking a pack a day.

They hate the way they look because they regularly treat themselves like someone they don't love. The way they look is just the reminder of a much more painful truth.

Try loving yourself instead.

Try finding things about yourself that are beautiful and cool and fun. The next time you catch yourself subconsciously reciting a list of your flaws, don't get angry at yourself: remember hate can't heal. Instead, just change the subject. Notice some good stuff instead.

Speak to yourself with love: *I love my eyes. I love the way I can make my friends laugh until we cry. I love how hard I work for my family. I'm proud of myself.*

Treat your body with love: a nice long bath with Strunz & Farah playing in the background, a slow walk on a chilly evening in your favorite hoodie, a massage if you can swing it, a good stretch every chance you get.

Change the conversation you have with yourself, and you will change the story you buy into.

Change the narrative you believe, and you will change the choices you make.

Change the way you treat yourself, and you will be more intentional about treating yourself with care.

What is your ~~ceiling~~ floor?

“Jeez, Mom, you’re such a snob.”

The child who just dropped that line is my oldest. Not yet eighteen, he’s somehow retained the ennui of a fading socialite since birth. But he’s still a teenager, and therefore he *knows everything.* *insert deep eye roll from me*

We were sitting at brunch on a family trip, and all three of my boys were teasing me. The target of their jokes? I wasn’t drinking my coffee.

Or to be more accurate, it’s fair to say I wasn’t drinking my coffee because I didn’t like the taste. I didn’t send the coffee back to the kitchen (it’s not the restaurant’s fault I’m not a fan of dark roast), but if the coffee wasn’t what I was hoping for, I’d rather not drink it.

Getting ribbed by my children is nothing new—our family has made a veritable art form out of banter—but something about Jackson’s comment hurt my feelings a little bit. He’d never called me a snob before, and some inner part of me began her dramatic soliloquy.

I’m a snob? Said the teenager eating overpriced avocado toast in a bougie eatery? Me? Who evolved from Folgers to McDonald’s coffee to Starbucks and then blazed right past to single-origin beans in a

Chemex? Me, who endlessly reheated the same cup of joe throughout each of their baby years but never actually managed to drink a warm cup in one sitting. And if, now, I have—through time and effort—refined my palate for these sacred beans, how does that make me a snob? This poser doesn't know anything about working your way up from AM/PM coffee!

And then I realize—that's the whole point.

My kid doesn't know any other way of living. He hasn't yet experienced decades of evolution—he's too young to look back and see how far he's come yet. Of course he doesn't understand something that took me decades to learn.

The quality of your life, literally the thing that decides the standard of your experience for each and every day, is not the height of your ceiling; it's the height of your floor.

Growing up I didn't grasp this at all. I'm a lifelong daydreamer with a vivid imagination. I've spent a good portion of my free time dreaming up plans and goals and future scenarios by the bucketload. As a young girl, I came to believe in the motto *If you can dream it, you can do it*. And so I thought my future experiences were only limited by my imagination and my willingness to work hard.

If the height of your "ceiling" (how vast you perceive your opportunities to be) is an open and endless sky that never stops expanding as long as you keep evolving, then anything might be possible. Your awareness of all that's available to you can inspire and encourage you to reach for more.

But then, if knowing our full potential were the only means to access our impact, we wouldn't have endless examples of people who persevered in spite of it. So many leaders and teachers and heroes in our history have created incredible things and reached unimaginable heights, despite the fact that they were never given "endless skies" of opportunity. So if your ceiling isn't the single determining factor in personal progress, what is?

Well if you ask me (she says, holding a delicious cup of pour-over coffee that's heated to a precise 130 degrees), what really, truly changes your life for the better is not adding more stars to your sky; it's adding more elevation to your earth.

When you stick your flag in the ground or draw a line in the sand and make a commitment to never, ever relinquish the ground you've gained—*that's what changes things forever.*

As far as I'm concerned, "Never again" is one of the most powerful statements in the English language. *Never again* happens when you're sick and tired of being sick and tired. It happens when you hit rock bottom and find the courage to stand back up. *Never again* says, "I'd rather be alone than allow someone to treat me like this." *Never again* says, "After working this hard to evolve, I commit to never *devolve.*" The absence of a ceiling means you can fly high, but the height of your floor determines the level you can bounce back from.

Before I learned this lesson, I used to circle back to the same negative experiences again and again. Different times, different places, different people even—but in hindsight, I was re-creating and reliving the same patterns over and over again. I'd use my imagination and arm myself with research and try countless ideas for how to fix this piece of me that seemed to be broken. It wasn't until I learned this truth that things began to change: you don't create your life based on what you imagine; you create your life based on what you *accept*. You teach people how to treat you by the way you treat yourself. Raising your floor is a reorientation of what you're willing to accept for yourself and your life.

And maybe it seems ridiculous to you, but I love coffee; it's one of my favorite things on earth. So if I'm going to love something this much, I really want to savor it. At this point in my life, I want it organic and single origin, and preferably roasted by a small local business, and served by a barista who is so precise with their tamper, I feel inferior just witnessing it. This isn't everyone's obsession—plenty of people couldn't care less about coffee. Legend has it there are some people who don't even drink coffee at all (and I will keep them in my prayers). But then I suppose they'll have a personal standard for something that's never even crossed my radar. That's the beauty of knowing the answers that matter most to you . . . you're living an experience that's totally unique.

I'm using coffee as my example, but I have all kinds of "floors" for the kind of life I want to create for myself and my children. I'm conscious of never going backward because it's such a slippery slope. We've all experienced that slope—when you're doing so well, you have great momentum, and then you're presented with one seemingly innocuous thing:

You *sure* you don't want a drink?
Can't you skip your workout just for today?
Come on, it's a party. Come outside and have a cigarette with me.
I miss you. Can we talk?
Oh, one piece of cake isn't gonna kill you!

Your sister isn't wrong—that one piece of cake won't kill you . . . neither will one drink or "one last night" with your toxic ex or the first cigarette after not touching one for eighteen months. None of those things, taken by themselves, is very dangerous. But breaking a promise you made to yourself mixed with the shame that comes with it coupled with a disruption in the momentum you've worked so hard to generate? That's an emotional shit storm.

Forget "falling off the wagon"; it doesn't take much to derail the whole train. That slipup to your plan is rarely "just one" of anything. It's opening a door that allows old bad habits to creep in followed by the voice in the back of your head that tells you all of the reasons you should just give up.

Sure, you can try again—your ceiling is high, and your possibilities are endless. But knowing that you can reach great heights isn't nearly as powerful as the faith that you will never sink to past depths again.

But, hey, isn't it just coffee . . . ?

For me, anything I consume as much as coffee will never be "just" anything.

I never really learned about true health or nutrition or living with vitality until I was in my midthirties. Until then I'd had such an awful relationship with what I thought healthy was. Growing up in the '80s/'90s, "healthy" was being on a diet: Atkins, South Beach, Master Cleanse, SlimFast, the Zone, Nutrisystem, Jenny Craig—my friends, family, and every magazine model tried them all. "Unhealthy" to my mind was anytime I wasn't on a diet, regardless of what I was actually consuming. I had no idea how all the highly processed, fake "food" I ate was affecting my health. Neither did anyone else I knew. I also didn't understand that once that junk food became a coping mechanism, I would attach so much more to it. Food became my favorite way to self-soothe—and I wasn't the first either. I saw the same story in my extended family going back generations. I'm guessing that for most families who grew up struggling to feed themselves like my ancestors sometimes did, fear around food scarcity and food insecurity gets passed down through the family tree like blue eyes or red hair. For my parents' generation, healthy living was a luxury they couldn't afford. In fact, in some seasons, food itself was a luxury they couldn't afford. That means that when they did have the money for it, food became much more than a commodity. Food became a treat and a source for celebration when times were good and an easy comfort when times were hard. A very long-winded way of saying to you that I spent the majority of my life eating absolute garbage, then feeling ashamed because of how I was living, then soothing those feelings with more junk food.

The cycle was vicious, and escaping it felt insurmountable after decades of trying. Ultimately, though, it wasn't a fad diet that helped me to change forever.

It was giving up soda.

Truly. Giving up soda in my thirties was the first "never again" decision I made for my health. I knew the chemicals in Diet Coke were awful for me, and for once I aimed to do what was best for my body rather than what might make me feel thin. It was a small change . . . so small I was certain it wouldn't really do much, but I wanted to see if I could keep my word to myself, since I'd never successfully given up anything before. Not having soda became my new standard—it was a small but firm platform I could start to build new healthy habits around.

Over a decade later, I cannot fathom my life back then. The food I ate, the sugar I consumed, the lack of sleep and water . . . *did I ever have fresh vegetables?* I'm not sure that I did!

I am now the queen of organic, the chancellor of slow food—ultraprocessed is my archnemesis. I care deeply about what I put in my body and what I feed my children because I understand now how vital our nutrition is for every part of our lives. I don't drink bad coffee because I can taste the difference now . . . my kids call it snobbery, but to me having coffee that isn't real feels like making a choice completely misaligned with who I am now.

A snob is someone who believes their tastes are superior to

other people's. I don't believe my choices should be the standard for anyone else.

My worst nightmare would be loving someone so much, I feel compelled to join them on a camping trip. But I have many friends who've experienced incredible world travel by staying at hostels and living off whatever food would keep in their backpack as they made their way across continents. They have the kind of once-in-a-lifetime stories about walking the Camino or backpacking through Cambodia, New Zealand, or Turkey. They've lived things that other people could never dream of—that's *their standard*. Their "floor" was the decision that finances would never stop them from seeing the world, and they haven't. We all have different baselines for how we'll enjoy nature, but our personal standards for the things we care about are the same for each of us.

I have similar standards for my work, my spiritual practice, the way I raise my children, and even my skincare routine. I have a minimum standard for every area of my life that matters to me. In fact, whenever I find that I'm not making progress in a certain area or feel like I keep repeating past mistakes, the answer is almost never that I need to dream bigger. The answer is that I need to shore up my bedrock and stop backsliding.

So my question for you in this moment is, Where do you need to elevate? Where do you need to raise your standards? Where do you need to plant a flag in the ground and *refuse* to keep giving up ground? Maybe it's something little and insignificant to the greater good (like my perfect cup of coffee), or maybe it's something that will shake up your community (like leaving a relationship that's unhealthy). Either way, when the floor you stand on elevates, everything in your life rises with it.

What's *working*?

I have been a podcast host for over seven years, and in that time, I've been able to interview all kinds of interesting people. I've spoken with presidents and chatted with Broadway stars. I've shared coffee talk with Oscar winners and star athletes. I've unpacked childhood trauma with everyone from CEOs to political activists.

On the show, we get into any topic and every topic. There's always laughter, sometimes tears, and more than one f-bomb has been dropped in pursuit of passionately driving a point across. I'm pretty proud of the fact that guests tend to open up during these conversations and we learn something new and fascinating. They'll share a little gossip about an ex or a secret tidbit about a new project. They tell me (and the audience) all kinds of interesting stories, but perhaps my absolute favorite thing someone can tell me is . . . *I've never told anyone this before.*

I don't just love that moment if it comes from a celebrity; I love that sentence coming from *anybody*. It's a pretty dramatic line, the kind of thing you hear at summer camp when you're twelve. If you're going to tell somebody something *you've never told anyone before??* It's got to be juicy, doesn't it?

We lean a little closer because this conversation just. got. real.

As a die-hard fan of podcasts, I find this type of episode the most exciting. A sexy rock star turns out to be extremely shy and awkward in real life? Delicious. The infamous world leader takes a hard left tangent away from nuclear disarmament to talk about how his mom used to bake him scones? Here for it! It's the best. But it really only happens when you're both truly following your curiosity and you're both in the moment.

So in order to keep it authentic and spontaneous, I don't prepare any questions in advance. I usually start with "How are you?" and then we meander away from there. But there is one question I end up asking almost every guest; it's the thing I'm most interested in knowing myself.

How did you get here?

I love this question. The answer is always varied and different and unique. Everyone has a journey, and the retelling of that story is augmented in *every way* by the person who recounts it. Mick Jagger will have a very different retelling of the Rolling Stones' journey than Keith Richards will. The Rolling Stones' manager or their longtime partners or children? They'll have entirely distinct perspectives on the same shared lifetime.

The stories people share are always different, yes, but I've begun to notice a similarity. Among the highest achievers and industry leaders, the people who have stayed at the top of their field for decades . . . something about their answer **is always the same**.

It's a mysterious sense of kismet, of serendipity, of right place / right time—and it always sends shivers up my spine. The first time I heard someone tell me a story like that, I was surprised. The man I was speaking with is one of the most successful actors of all time, but his first big break into Hollywood was almost a happy accident. He was in the exact right place at the exact right time—and he got cast in the role that changed his career by simply acting like, well, himself.

The second time someone told this type of story it was so similar that I got chills. Again and again, I heard story after story with the same patterns. The wildly successful start-up founder who sold her company for a billion dollars? She was an intern at a massive corporation. She got randomly assigned to an executive who—unbeknownst to anybody at the time—was about to leave to start their own company. That executive hired his intern to be his new assistant—later the assistant would work her way up. Eventually they'd become business partners in a venture that would change both their lives forever.

Sure, that woman worked her butt off—in fact, that's something that also rings true for every successful person I've talked with no matter what industry they're in. But that kid *just so happened* to get placed as an intern with a man who had funding already in place to start his own business. That same VC firm would later support their joint start-up. She jumped a line some people never get to the front of no matter how hard they work, how smart they might be, or how deserving they are.

Then there was the comedian who stayed open and excited—he said yes to everything. This little gig led to that one with slightly more people in the audience. That little comedy club connected him with another where he'd meet the manager who would help him get to the next level. He spent fifteen years on the road doing comedy clubs before the public ever knew his name. Now he sells out stadiums.

I've heard versions of this story so many times now, I swear I can feel them coming before the guest even gets to the punchline. My antennae go up, and my whole being pays attention. My intuition taps me on the shoulder: *Rach, this is something important.*

When I think about all of these conversations, it really does seem like they're all sharing the same recipe for success. And if an equation for progress exists that transcends industries, countries, ages, genders, socioeconomic backgrounds—literally everything—then we should for sure pay attention!

Here it is:

1. Get really, really excited about something **you enjoy doing**.
2. Practice the thing you're excited about and fall in love with the *process*.
3. Be on the lookout for an opportunity to grow in the thing you're excited about.
4. Say yes to *every* opportunity as long as it's related to the thing you're excited about.
5. Put ZERO time limit on achieving success and focus fully on the process of becoming better.
6. Say yes to every opportunity that will elevate your new level of skill around the thing you're excited about.
7. Win, lose, or draw: every opportunity will lead to bigger opportunities around the thing you're excited about.
8. Go back to step one. Repeat forever.

Freaking epic! I vibe the hell out of this road map because it feels so organic. If you've experienced success in a certain area of your life, I'm sure you can see similarities in your own path. OK, *but here's the thing*, it's often unspoken, but it's something I read between the lines and get as answers to all the follow-up questions I ask them in order to better understand.

None of them used force.

Not one truly successful person I've interviewed forced their success in *any* way. In fact, most of them would tell you that their biggest career failures or the times their companies came close to bankruptcy were always the result of them trying to make something happen when every indication, intuition, and insight they had told them it wasn't a good fit.

Perhaps I find this so astounding because the achiever in me spent so many years believing I could will my way to success. I believed if I would just work harder or put in more hours, I could make an idea into something real. And the thing is, I did.

But I have always experienced those opportunities and career successes hand in hand with product launches that flopped like dying fish. Because these things happened simultaneously and because I was moving so fast, I never slowed down to ask myself **what was working** and, when it didn't—why it failed.

Looking back, I realize that every major success I've had—**y'all, literally every single one**—followed that recipe I've listed above.

Writing books? I do it because I love it . . . the success wasn't fast in coming, but I didn't care because I was so pumped that I got to write books that someone (anyone!) wanted to read. It didn't come easy—stringing words together is a lonely slog, and it always will be, but easy or hard, I keep at it because I like the process.

Hosting a podcast? Same exact thing. I never even looked at my podcast numbers for years—I literally didn't even know how to access them. I just made the content because I liked it. Seven years and over two hundred million downloads later—it involved a lot of work, but I never had to force it to be successful; it just was.

Public speaking and producing conferences? It was slow and steady, and I was just doing it because I loved it. Then it was a snowball rolling down the hill so fast, I had no idea how to control it.

All of my career success happened when I flowed with opportunity instead of trying to force it to appear.

But if I'm going to tell you about my wins, I have to tell you that there were a lot of failures where I tried to force the funk. I'd expend loads of time and money and (most important) energy and focus on things that would rob me of whole years of effort with nothing to show for it. Meanwhile, my big three—writing, podcast, live talks—would just keep rolling along. It was a living definition of the 80/20 principle.

It wasn't until I heard other people begin to speak about this that I was able to see these patterns. Then I couldn't help but wonder . . . what would happen if I only put energy and time and focus into things that naturally flowed for me? What if I started every new project with intention but paid extreme *attention* to whether or not it was unfolding without force?

I've stopped putting effort into pushing things uphill. Don't get me wrong, it absolutely **can** be done. You can force your way in and outhustle everyone and make it happen—I've spoken with a lot of rich people who've done just that. But 100 percent of the time, those people have an aura of chaos; their vibration is frenetic and distorted. I've yet to meet a single one, no matter how much money they have, who has a quality of life that inspires me.

If your measure of success right now is financial, I totally get it. Money can't buy happiness, but it can pay your rent and your phone bill and take a massive amount of worry off your shoulders. Money can make your life a hell of a lot easier, and I'll never begrudge anyone who tries to improve their financial means because that was my story as well. But for what it's worth, please note that I said I've met a lot of *rich* people who've forced their way ahead, but I've never met a wealthy one.

Rich isn't permanent. But wealth—*true wealth*—means you are so financially secure, it can't be taken away. So it's worth mentioning that the successful people I've met who learned to go with the flow . . . they aren't rich.

They're wealthy. And chill as hell about it too.

Now back to you. Even if financial independence isn't your goal, chances are you've got at least one goal or you wouldn't still be reading this book. I would love to save you the forty years it took me to figure this out. I'd love to save you the wasted time and money and energy I've lost along the way and ask you to consider, **What's working?**

In your life, your career, your relationships—what works? What flows smoothly and easily? Which parts of your world, even though they still require work and effort, do you always find new opportunities and experiences you appreciate?

I think I've mentioned the Pareto principle in almost every nonfiction book I've written, but I never stop being impressed by how helpful the concept is. Vilfredo Pareto (besides having a fabulously rhymey name) was an Italian economist living in the late 1800s. He realized that 80 percent of the land in Italy was owned by only 20 percent of its citizens. Then he realized something similar was happening in his garden: 80 percent of the harvest was produced by roughly 20 percent of his crop. When studied, this same percentage breakdown shows up again and again. 20 percent of your customers are responsible for 80 percent of your revenue. 20 percent of your actions are giving you 80 percent of your results. The goal to more success or health or improvement—or even just less discomfort—is to try to figure out which 20 percent is giving you the best results and focus more on that.

But what if it's really just that 20 percent of what we do is guided by something bigger than us? What if that 20 percent accounts for God or spirit guides or your Great-Aunt Sara working as a guardian angel or *whatever*, and they're opening the exact doors you're meant to walk through at the exact right time? What if some things come easy because it's the route you're supposed to take? What if some things don't work out at all because the universe is trying to tell you that he's not your Prince Charming; he's a fuckboy, and you need to move on?

By paying attention to what is working in your life and leaning more heavily in that direction, at the very least, you'll experience less tension and stress and anxiety. You'll flow more easily from one opportunity to the next, and I have a sneaking suspicion you just might experience the most success (and the most contentment) you ever have.

How are you *really*?

Admittedly, this isn't a question I get very often.

My boo is never like, "Baby, how are you? I can't tell."

He can always tell.

I'm not very good at hiding what I'm feeling or *how* I'm feeling—even if I'm trying to. *I think, therefore I am* . . . one giant ball of emotion at any given moment. If I'm happy, everyone knows it. If I'm upset, I get really quiet, but still, nobody in the immediate vicinity would assume it's a good time to strike up a conversation or pitch me on taking a personality test to find out if I'm a good fit for Scientology.

I'm pretty up front about my emotions (for better or worse), but I'm popping this question in here because I recognize that not everybody is.

The aforementioned "boo" at the top of the page? He's a grade-A, stoic-level, *work-it-out-on-your-own-and-don't-bother-anyone-with-your-feelings* kind of human. An incredible characteristic to have when you're handling the career of an artist—the only one in the room allowed to freak out—not so great when your partner is big on expressing her feelings and is gonna require the same from you. This is one hell of a new skill to adopt in your midforties, and hat tip to him for being willing to step outside his comfort zone in order to be in a relationship with a verbal processor. I'd like to think that his willingness to learn a new communication style has also shifted his internal dialogue and maybe—just maybe—has allowed this very capable, self-reliant, grown man who handles everything for everyone else to give himself a little more grace around those times when, you know what, no, he's actually ***not*** *OK.*

For today's purposes, I'd like to propose that's what you and I do.

Let's pretend we're dating. I'm your new girlfriend, and, yes, that means you've now got to manage someone with the emotional whims of a prize racehorse, *but also*, lucky you, I am both hilarious *and* incredible in the sack.

Sometimes both at the same time.

In this scenario, we're out on a date at our favorite natural wine bar, and for once, the club next door isn't playing house music at 4 p.m. on a Saturday, so we can actually hear each other talk. The purveyor of this groovy establishment—a bearded ginger by the name of Matt—has just poured us a glass of orange wine and given us a five-minute monologue on its provenance and the artist responsible for the label art. As Matt meanders away, you relax into comfortable repose ready for lighthearted chitchat. Ah, but you forgot who you're dating, and I'm going to jump in before you can even comment on how mild the weather is.

So how are you—really?

Human instinct is usually to—consciously or not—take this question as meaningless. We assume it's a polite way of making conversation. But what I'd love for you to consider from this moment forward is that this question, anytime you hear it or any of its kin, is coming straight from the universe. It's coming straight from God in Her infinite wisdom. It's being asked by your guardian angels, your ancestors, or whatever other force you believe in.

How are you? Is an essential, soul-searching inquiry. *How are you?* is something that few people will ever slow down long enough to consider.

Now don't get me wrong, being able to slow down and ask yourself deeper questions is a privilege that not everyone will experience. My grandmother was a migrant farm worker with limited education and six children to raise and was married to an alcoholic. I imagine she spent decades living in fight-or-flight mode, and her only focus most of the time would have been whether her family had food on the table. She wasn't slowing down long enough (if ever) to check in with herself—she wouldn't have had the knowledge or the language to consider such a thing.

But my instinct is that if you're taking the time to read or listen to this book, you *do* have the occasional opportunity to slow down and consider how you are. Or at the very least you've become aware that you *must* slow down and consider how you are because you can't keep going on the way you have been.

So . . . how are you, really?

Yeah, I'm going to keep asking it over and over like that scene in *Good Will Hunting*. I'll keep asking until something cracks through the veneer and the question permeates deep. Not because I want you to break open and break down and have a good cry (unless that's what you need) but because I just want you to be real with yourself too. Because chances are, if you don't ask this question of yourself regularly, it's likely that *how you think you are* has a lot more to do with the people around you and how they expect you to be.

If everyone around you is positive and happy (or at the very least, their social media makes them seem that way), you'll naturally portray those emotions, even if they're not authentic to you. You'll learn to fake it, you'll learn to pretend, and worse still, you'll start to internalize the idea that something must be wrong with you because you're not as OK as you're pretending to be.

The opposite is also permeating the lives of every single person I know who's under the age of thirty. Whether it's my younger friends in their midtwenties or my children in their teens, I've watched a massive increase in the conversations surrounding anxiety over the last few years. As someone who has suffered from PTSD and anxiety for decades, I was quick to take note of it because—at first—I thought it was so cool that a younger generation was talking about mental health and how to treat it. Then I began to notice my teenagers and their friends used the word "anxiety" to describe *everything.*

Oh my God, I have a test tomorrow. I'm literally having an anxiety attack—this from a friend of my son. All the sixteen-year-olds at our monthly Full Moon Dinner agreed, their "anxiety" was really going off about this test.

I thought about walking up to the girl at the bar, but my anxiety took over and I chickened out. That one is from one of my guy friends in his early twenties.

I began to notice it so much, I started to dig in with them.

What does it feel like when you have anxiety? What happens in your body? What happens in your mind?

Turns out, they were experiencing nerves. Literally just nerves.

Sometimes the nerves were negative, and sometimes they were genuinely excited over something great, but in each instance, they identified the feeling as anxiety because they've heard it used so often. Because they identified the feeling as anxiety, and because they've heard the signs and symptoms discussed so often, they'd pull away from others, isolate themselves, or remove themselves from situations altogether because they were positive the anxiety was going to grow into an "attack." The cute boy in his twenties canceled on several potential dates because he was positive the uncomfortable feeling he had was going to get worse. It took a long while and many heart-to-hearts with people over the age of forty before he realized that there are some situations (like putting yourself out there as a single person) that will always feel uncomfortable because they're outside your comfort zone. But if you aren't familiar with those feelings, and everyone around you is labeling themselves and labeling you, it's too easy to just accept their reality if you haven't checked in with yourself to see how you are.

Sometimes you'll check in and discover that you're actually struggling in a certain way, and that makes for a beautiful opportunity to practice self-love and self-care.

Sometimes you'll check in with yourself and realize that you've been feeling really negative and bitter lately (or sad and worried lately or stressed out in the extreme lately), but some soul searching will reveal it's not how your authentic self is feeling. Sometimes your feelings are based more on *proximity* than reality. Meaning, those feelings might be there because you've been spending too much time with people who are living in a lower vibrational state, and you need to get some space from them before you can settle back into your true feelings.

Sometimes you'll check in with yourself and become aware, possibly for the first time, that you're really quite content with your life and exactly where you need to be in this moment. I had coffee with a work acquaintance recently who was relaying her family's obsession with her chosen career. She is a freelancer in the creative field rather than choosing medicine like all of her siblings. In her culture, she told me, only certain industries are acceptable. Anything else is less than. Her parents and siblings were doing everything in their power to convince her she was on the wrong track. They'd recently had a big family meeting to discuss her choice to be a freelance creative, and she came away from that call feeling so discouraged.

Y'all, she is a grown woman with incredible skills who is successfully supporting herself working at something she loves. Beyond that, she's a total badass and truly excellent at her job (I met her through her work), and yet she finds herself in a situation where the people she loves are telling her she "shouldn't be this happy" if she's not driving a luxury car or making the same amount of money they are. It'd be much easier to ignore those voices if they weren't attached to people she knows care about her, even if they don't understand her. Can any of you relate?

The really beautiful awareness to come out of that very difficult conversation with her family is that she was more resolved than ever with her truth.

"I'm happy," she told me. "I really enjoy what I do, and I love that I don't work long hours or nights and weekends. I don't want to live to work; I want to work to support the life I want to have. I'm actually doing great."

For someone less confident or someone who isn't actually in touch with their true feelings, it would be so easy to get wound up in the fears and opinions of her family. That kind of energy can completely derail a life that is on the exact right course—even if it doesn't make sense to other people.

The point in asking this question is, yes, so you'll check in with yourself right now in this moment. But it's also to encourage you to ask yourself this question regularly and for the rest of your life. As your girlfriend, I want the best for you, and that's only possible if you know yourself.

Did you win, or did you learn?

You want to know the secret to long-term success?

No BS, no special hack, no magic cure, no course to buy . . . just the absolute truth about achieving success in any area of your life?

Not giving up.

That's it.

It's tenacity. It's consistency. It's ten thousand hours practicing in the dark for every one hour you're celebrated in the spotlight. It's becoming an overnight success after a lifetime of working at something.

And, yes, I know I told you this is a book of questions, not one full of my answers—but this answer isn't just and only mine. It's the answer for every athlete, every superstar, every business hero, every iconoclast, every great person in the history of the world, *and all of the evil ones too*.

Read their biographies *or their obituaries*. Study history. They're the ones who never gave up, the ones who found a way, the ones who kept going in spite of the opposition, the critics, and the setbacks.

It's Kobe reminding us that "boos don't block shots."

It's Edison finding "9,999 ways ***not*** to make a lightbulb."

It's the old-school agent fighting for Tina Turner when everyone said she was over . . . "Once a star," he told them, "always a threat."

There are a million stories of successful people and businesses and revolutionaries *not* giving up when all of the evidence told them they should. If you haven't seen this theme repeated throughout history again and again, then might I suggest that you're not paying attention to the most important part of the success story?

I can't blame you for that though—we're all taught to focus on the athletes crossing the finish line, not the years they spent in training for the race.

The training is boring and unglamorous. The training involves blisters and tears and failures piled high. If people watched our version of training, they might realize that a good majority of the time, we had no idea what we were doing. Far from being experts in our field, our relationships, and even our own kitchen—if people watched our "training," they'd soon discover we're making a lot of it up as we go along.

Have you ever seen those videos of world-famous athletes playing their sport back when they were "just OK" at it? Have you ever heard Ed Sheeran's early song recordings? Or Adele's? Or the footage of Oprah when she was a young news anchor? Watching a modern-day superstar back when they were still "in training" is the most affecting example of the fact that, well, everybody sucks in the beginning. Even people with natural talent in one area had to grow themselves into different parts of their industry in order to compete at the highest levels. And even the people who developed unmatched and unparalleled skill—even that isn't enough.

Being the best at what you do isn't enough.

Even the best get knocked down, make mistakes, or have a bad season. The truly successful, the ones who stand the test of time . . . *they* had to develop an unshakable mindset along with their undisputed skill.

Please see: Taylor Swift and the Eras Tour, Michael Jordan coming back from a failed stint in baseball to win three more championships, or basically anything Robert Downey Jr. did after 1996.

Success isn't about short-lived intensity; it's about long-term consistency.

The slipup, the slowdown, the decision (or indecision) that took you wildly off course? That wasn't the end of the line for you . . . that was just an obstacle put in your path to make you strong enough for the journey you've embarked on.

The question for you to ask before you begin something new is not *Do I have what it takes to start this project?* The question should be *Do I have what it takes to start this project again and again and again?*

I've never heard of a single successful person who has only encountered easy roads with ideal results 100 percent of the time. Have you? Of course not! If you're being real with yourself, you know that the path to success looks a lot like failure most of the time . . . so why on earth do you get discouraged when you encounter it in your life?

Because it'd be so much nicer if it wasn't so freaking hard.

Because *knowing* that some kind of hardship might happen is very different from the actual unprecedented reality that real life throws at us.

When my kids went to summer camp for the first time, I was terrified of them being away from home for two weeks without me. I worried about them getting homesick. I worried about the lack of air-conditioning at camp. I worried about my little boy getting bullied by big kids. I worried about my big boy sneaking to the girl's camp and trying to make out with someone.

I worried about *everything*.

You know what I never worried about? Ford (age seven) getting upset with another boy in his cabin and trying (thankfully in vain) to bite off that boy's big toe.

What the hell?!

In all my parenting career, I'd never had a kid get in trouble for attacking another kid's hoof—and yet there I was on the phone with a camp counselor telling me about how Ford really needed to better manage his emotions.

Life is wild. The plan will go to hell in a handbasket at least half the time. I think the reason things can be so overwhelming to us is because we weren't planning on *that particular* kind of problem, whatever it was. We thought our setback would look like our friend Sara's. We thought our relationship problems would be more like our brother and his wife. We had all these examples—except the ones that actually showed up. So when they did show up for us, we assumed the overall unique disaster we encountered must be because we're so terrible at the things we're pursuing.

But, dude, you are a totally original little weirdo ... why wouldn't your failures be too?

It's all part of it.

Every single day that flows perfectly, every single day that feels impossible—it's all part of it. Every single workout that feels awesome, every single workout that feels like four tons of crap—it's all part of it. Every single customer that's thrilled with your work, every single customer that hates the product—it's all part of it. Making the money, losing the money, getting your dream job, burning the cake—it's all part of it. Meeting the man of your dreams *and then meeting his beautiful wife*? (Thank you, Alanis!) It's all part of it.

The question is not what happened to you; the question is, What have you decided it means?

You didn't fail, you just learned 9,999 ways not to make a lightbulb.

In fact, if you want to succeed you must stop looking at *anything* as a failure.

Either we win or we learn.

Either we achieve the thing we were trying to achieve or we learn the lesson we need to win the point next time. You have to look at life that way. You have to look at business that way. You have to look at your health that way. Life either goes how you want it to go or unfolds how it *needs to* in order to better help you succeed in the future.

If you're unhappy with how a particular area is unfolding, ask yourself what lesson you need to learn to play the game better next time. But for goodness' sake, don't leave the field just because you struck out! Reggie Jackson struck out 2,597 times, and he's in the Hall of Fame! When was the last time you failed at something 2,597 times? In fact, let's make a rule . . . let's all agree that we're no longer allowed to give up at something until we've "failed" at it as much as Reggie Jackson.

Until then, let's ask a great question . . . did I win, or did I learn? If you won, ask yourself why and how and what variables were present to create that result . . . and then **do them again and again**. If you learned, same questions. How and why and what variables were present to create that result? And then **never repeat that particular combination**.

I know it's hard to do the thing you're trying to do, but you've figured out other hard things before, I know you have!

When I was in the sixth grade, I went to an amusement park with the other girls of Troop 723. (Shout-out to the Girl Scouts!) I grew up in a small town, and besides recreational drug use, there were *very* few stimulating activities for kids.

Getting to go to Magic Mountain?

It was the jam! For a group of small-town, awkward tweens, getting to go to Six Flags was like attending the Met Gala as a guest of Anna Wintour: it doesn't get better. We'd happily sold cookies and wrapping paper and participated in the marching band car wash—literally anything to get on the bus that would drive us a couple hours through the canyon to an amusement park with our friends.

I had so looked forward to that trip, and it would have been fantastic, except that my period decided to show up the day before. I had only gotten my period for the first time a few months earlier, and I was still driving blind. My sole initiation to menstruation was my mother singsonging "Welcome to womanhood!" and then promptly never speaking to me about it again. I had no idea how to use the pads my two older sisters kept under the bathroom sink, and I was way too embarrassed to ask.

Trying to figure out how to use a pad without any professional guidance looks a little like a chimpanzee attempting to use a computer for the first time. If you've never seen one before (a pad, I mean; obviously you've seen a chimpanzee), it sort of looks like a clamshell. You open it up, and one side has a cotton layer to catch the blood, and the other side is sticky, sort of like fly paper—it's what makes the pad stick to your chonies. Some pads also have wings that make it extra secure, but I assumed those were for rich people because I never saw one in our house.

It took me a minute to figure out the pad, but I got there eventually. Or at least I thought I did. Until that trip to Magic Mountain.

Somewhere between the entry gate and the first roller coaster, I became very aware that something had gone very wrong in the pad department. While standing in line for Colossus, I started to feel a sharp pain all along the surface of my vulva.

Oh my God, I realized with horror, *my pubic hair is stuck in the sticky part of the pad!*

I tried surreptitiously doing a side lunge to detach myself, but that only made it worse. How did this happen? What did I do wrong? Did it detach? Did the whole front flap fold in on itself and trap my sparse pube collection like a mouse trap?

I couldn't figure out the error of my ways, but I also wasn't about to get out of the line to figure it out. Waiting for a roller coaster on a hot summer day could take upward of eleven hours, so leaving was too great a risk. I decided to brazen it out and hope that whatever was happening with my pad would at least still catch the blood, lest I be embarrassed by a leak on top of the unintentional bikini wax I was getting every time I stepped forward in line.

The hour it took to get to the front of that line was so painful. I tried not moving unless absolutely necessary, but my pubes still hurt. I tried casually stretching or moving on the sly—literally everything I could think of that might help me get unstuck. I dreaded going to the bathroom to discover whatever disaster awaited me in my pants.

Finally, blessedly, I made my way into a stall and pulled down my pants (very, *very* carefully) to discover . . . nothing at all.

Nothing was out of sorts. I hadn't just accidentally scalped myself down below. There was nothing amiss. Not so much as a single hair out of place. I sat on the toilet for the longest time, absolutely confounded. If all the hair hadn't just been ripped out of my vulva, then what on earth was going on?

What was going on is that I was having cramps.

I'd never had them before. This was the early '90s, and in the commercials on TV, the women were always holding their stomach, so I assumed cramps happened somewhere around the belly button. No idea whatsoever that they could show up directly on your labia . . . and inside your vagina and your boobs, your lower back, and, much to my chagrin, very intensely inside and around your butthole.

I was having cramps, but I was too afraid to ask anyone what was going on, so for a couple of years—*years*—I thought that my pads were pulling on my pubes. In fact, it wasn't until I began using tampons and it still happened that I finally realized something else was amiss.

Figuring out your hormones, your cycle, and your period is so confusing—I'm still navigating it in my forties. But *I did* figure it out because I understand that it's an essential part of my life.

Beyond your period and even beyond your body, you will have so many examples of doing the same—figuring out the things you needed to figure out to get to where you wanted to go. Whether it was college or parenting or to Magic Mountain with the rest of Troop 723.

This dream you're chasing, it's no different. You'll try stuff, it won't always work, you'll (hopefully) try something else. It's never a question of whether or not you're capable because with enough time and effort, anyone can be. It's always a question of how much time and effort you're willing to put in to get yourself across that finish line.

What would you do if you knew you **could not ~~fail~~ succeed?**

OK, this one isn't my question—this one comes from the place most great one-liners come from: Seth Godin.

And, yes, I did already mention him in this book, but this is such a great freaking question, I want to buy real estate there. I mean, we've all heard the question *What would you do if you knew you could not fail?* The idea surrounding that one is basically, *Don't be afraid; do the thing you really want to do*. The way to figure out what you really want to do? You ask yourself what you'd pursue if you knew that victory was guaranteed. It's a beautiful way to live life, and I highly recommend it as a tool for being honest with yourself. But this question from Seth, this flips the whole thing on its head.

*What would you do if you knew you **would** fail?*

Said another way—which pursuit would make you so damn happy just to be involved in (or even scantily adjacent to it) that you'd do it with or without success? The first question asks you to identify what kind of goal is worth pursuing.

This question asks you what kind of life is worth living.

I realized I was falling in love with my partner long before I even knew if he was attracted to me. We were friends and had bonded over the fact that we weren't looking for romantic partners, only buddies. But one day I looked up at him, and it was like someone hit my heart with a sledgehammer. I skated right past the crush stage and went headlong into *I'm going to love this man for the rest of my life.*

It was absolutely horrifying.

My previous relationship had been long and deeply unhealthy, and I had zero ability to trust another man. Also, it's important to add that the object of my affection was essentially a lone wolf. At forty-four years old, he was single, had never been married, and never had children—and never planned to. He'd spent the previous twenty years circumnavigating the globe with rock stars and loved his nomadic lifestyle. He told me once—because we were just friends—that while he'd loved very deeply, he wasn't sure he'd ever really been "in love." And because we were *just friends*, I was like, "Yeah, I can totally understand that . . ."

But then all of the sudden my heart exploded, and all of the confetti were teeny, tiny pieces of paper with his name hand-lettered on each and every one. So to top off every other overwhelming feeling, I was now dead-deep in love with someone who'd "never been in love."

Jesus wept.

I agonized over this reality for weeks and weeks. I made myself sick trying to talk my stupid heart out of these feelings. I made a playlist, eponymously titled ***In My Feels***, filled with songs like "Strong Enough" by Sheryl Crow and "Insensitive" by Jann Arden. This poor man didn't even *know* I was having a full dramatic breakdown (with accompanying soundtrack!) each night after I put my kids to bed. But the resolution I came to after weeks and weeks of being full-blown emo was an awareness of two important things.

One, I really was in love with him. I could not talk myself out of it, no matter how hard I tried. And two, loving him was *my* truth—even if he never loved me back.

That was the awareness that allowed my soul to settle, and after weeks of insomnia, I finally got some sleep. I loved him, and it wasn't contingent. It was worth loving him even if that love was only ever one-sided. Whether I knew him for a couple of months or a year—or forever, as it turns out—it was worth it to me to tell the truth about how I was feeling no matter what the consequences. It was worth it to me to "fail" at the actual relationship with him as long as it meant I was able to be true to myself.

The next time we hung out, he must have seen it in my eyes—I'm sure I looked like a cartoon bunny who'd just spied a giant carrot. I was oozing love. Radioactive with it. He started to get sort of twitchy; he looked concerned. At some point he began to babble about feelings and not wanting me to get hurt: "I mean, not, obviously, that you're feeling any kind of way. I just want to be honest and—"

I remember smiling so huge because I was totally grounded in that moment. My smile stopped his monologue midsentence.

"I'm in love with you," I told him.

He froze like I'd just pulled a gun.

"And I'm not telling you that because I expect anything back. I'm telling you because it's true. I'm telling you because life is short, and if I got hit by a bus tomorrow, I'd want you to know that I died loving you."

OK, I'm dramatic. So what?

He stared at me in utter shock, not speaking—I'm not even sure if he was *breathing*. And then . . .

"Fuuuuuuuuuck," he groaned. He said it with every ounce of worry and fear he possessed. If I'm psychoanalyzing here—and of course I am—it was the culmination of emotions after decades of avoiding this exact kind of entanglement.

And I just kept right on smiling because expressing myself wasn't for him—it was for me. I gave him a hug.

"Don't worry," I assured him. "It will all be OK."

And it is—way better than OK. It's the most loving, beautiful, supportive, authentic relationship I've ever known in my life. Once upon a time, I thought that if you'd found a deep love, that it was guaranteed to last forever—I'm older now, and I understand that we don't work that way. People grow (hopefully) and change (ideally for the better), and it's possible that even with a deep love, at some point you won't be compatible as romantic partners anymore.

Maybe he gets a full lobotomy and forgets that he loves me, and I have to *Notebook* him every single day to remind him. Maybe he meets a backup singer named Sheila and decides that she's foxier and cooler than I am (as if!) and moves on. Paul Simon told us there were fifty ways to leave a lover, but it's probably an infinite number. Regardless of how many ways this could go wrong, it would be worth it to me for everyday it went *right*.

What's worth pursuing even if it doesn't end perfectly?

A friend of mine is an artist who experienced a lot of success in the past and then lost her intention. It happens to the best of us. She started chasing wins instead of creative expression (been there too). A long season of that kind of uncertainty, especially after so much time creating in a flow state, really messes with your head. Ideally, yes, we are supposed to separate ourselves from our work, but for artists, their work is an extension of them. If suddenly nobody likes the art, or at least they don't like it *as much*, it's pretty damn hard not to internalize that as nobody liking *you*. The existential crisis came careening in from every direction. Because now she's in a full spiral—*Is this even what I want to make? Is this who I even am? Did I just make this because I thought they'd like it? Did I only begin to make art in the first place because I thought they'd like me?*

When I first heard Seth's question, she was the first one I called. "Flip it," I urged her. "Go small. Go teeny, tiny. Go back to the most basic level. Which part of your work would you still pursue even if nobody saw it? Even if everybody saw it and they all hated it? Which pieces would you do purely for the love of the game?"

Our culture is so obsessed with external success. I've been a victim of that belief—that if I was admirable in the eyes of others, then I was good and right and *worthy*. And this is not some bid to say that pursuing success is wrong—my pursuit of success is how I pay for my family to live. And, yes, money will never buy your happiness—but it *will* pay rent and put gas in your car and pay for braces for your kid. So as much as it's not a key, it's freaking *helpful* in making your life more comfortable. But the external success the world seems to be so focused on is the accumulation of admiration. Somewhere along the road to this pursuit, we stop playing to win and start obsessing over how *not to lose*. We begin to augment our work, our life, even our bodies in pursuit of what we think other people will like. As an artist or creator or leader, this decision is the beginning of the end of your unique magic, the very thing that would have made you special. Worse than that, it's a surefire way to lose the only kind of success that actually matters to our soul, the internal kind. The joy of finishing the project of your heart. The contentment in a job well done. The peace in knowing that you honor yourself by *being* yourself.

What's totally ironic too is that most external success happens when we're aligned internally. When we're not pursuing something for any other reason than that it's what our soul most longs for.

Your pursuit should feel authentic to you, but it doesn't have to be some grandiose thing that changes the world. It just has to be something that makes your heart happy. Recently I watched an hour-long tutorial about the correct application of concealer versus foundation—I had no idea the intricacies of this process. I had no idea someone could teach and demonstrate it for a full hour! The woman on YouTube was deeply passionate about the topic, and I was thoroughly riveted, even though I rarely wear makeup and don't own a single one of the one thousand brushes she used to do the job. She didn't have a ton of subscribers to her channel, but that particular video had *millions* of views. She didn't strike me as someone who was trying to please the world; she seemed to me to be a woman who absolutely loved the artistry in what she did. She seemed to me like the kind of person who would—and maybe does—talk about her passion to anybody willing to listen. She's speaking her truth (which incidentally is that concealer goes on before foundation, of which I had no idea) regardless of what the outcome is.

In case you haven't realized it yet, this pursuit is the only possible win-win scenario. There is absolutely no guarantee that anything you put out into the world will be well received by others. Maybe they'll hate it. Maybe they won't notice it at all. But if you made something you love *and* you loved the making of it—then the outcome doesn't actually matter. In fact, you'll be so in love and passionate about what you're doing, you won't even wait around to see what the public reaction was. You'll just move onto the next thing that feels inspiring and good to your soul: it's very David Bowie of you. Sometimes that means you'll spend years living in

East Berlin doing dark portraits of Germans who don't know that you're a rock star, and other times it means you'll accidentally create your most successful album on your fifteenth attempt. You'll sell ten million copies of that album—not because you were trying but because you were experimenting.

How old are "you" right now?

Ever been wildly triggered about something *so insignificant*, you can't comprehend why it set you off?

Same.

Most memorably, I once had a debilitating anxiety attack—the kind that swallows a whole day with nausea, shaking, an elephant of pressure crushing my chest—all because someone I barely knew sounded "stern" on a phone call.

Stern. That's it. That's all that happened. He "sounded stern," and I had an emotional meltdown.

I could tell you fifty more memories just like that one.

These experiences don't happen during seasons of emotional distress. They occur when everything is chill. One moment I'm fine, the next I'm suffocating inside an emotional cyclone. There's no warning shot, no external variables that create the perfect storm for a breakdown—in fact, I rarely notice the moment I'm triggered. It's only afterward, in the nose dive, that I'm aware something set me off.

In the course of my adult life, I've been triggered into a psychological spiral, into binge eating, and into drinking to get drunk. I've been triggered into obsessive circular thinking, into manic episodes, and into low-grade depression. But of all possible outcomes, the worst and most common result for me is anxiety.

Severe anxiety feels like being trapped inside a terror I can't escape. In those instances, I don't have anxiety; **I am anxiety**. Every worry, every awful thought, every possible catastrophe—they're absolutely real. Another rational adult might try to talk me down, explain how the grandiose scenario I'm panicking about isn't likely to occur. But my body is involved now. My heart is racing, and my stomach is sick, so it's hard to believe someone who reassures me that *nothing is happening*. Clearly, it's happening. I can feel it, right now, inside of me.

Over time, I learned that if I could create even the smallest bit of space from the feelings in my body, I could use that pocket of air to dig my way out.

The first "pocket of air" I discovered was understanding that what I was feeling wasn't permanent. Because it came on without warning and went away eventually, I could cling to the ephemeral nature of the experience. If it was temporary, it made sense to me *that something must be making the anxiety happen.*

That's when I first learned about emotional triggers. A trigger is a catalyst for a severe emotional response, regardless of your current mood. Bingo! There was a name for what was happening to me. I could dig myself out by a few more inches.

Identifying ***when*** my mood shifted allowed me to dig out a bit more. *I was fine this morning and great during the day, but just after lunchtime, something shifted . . .* I would run the moment back in my mind. I'm unsure if it's like that for others, but I often wouldn't know which component unsettled me until I played it back. It's like watching a movie. Everything I'm "watching" is fine until one moment when it's suddenly not OK. My whole body reacts viscerally. Freeze frame. It could be a face, a tone of voice, a song that was playing, a particular smell . . . anything.

It's like finally seeing the monster under the bed—yes, it's still scary, but at least now you know what you're up against. Understanding ***what*** I was triggered by became my greatest hack for separating myself from anxiousness. It might still haunt me, but at least I could name it, make it less corporal. "You're not real," I'd tell it. "You're only here because the car backfired, and the sound reminded me of that day, and that made me feel scared . . ."

Once I figured out the trigger, I could usually see the correlation with an unhappy memory from my past. Other triggers I can identify but have never uncovered why they terrify me so much: crossing a long bridge by car or the look of certain apartment buildings—they remind me of something, just on the edge of memory. I'm not keen to excavate these tender bits. It's enough, for now, to know that something about them causes suffering.

Early on in my self-work, this was one of the greatest tools I had in my toolkit. If I could identify what the trigger *was*, it gave me a certain amount of power over it. Understanding what set me off became my obsession. At least if I knew that piece of information, I could separate myself from the feeling.

But while I knew what a trigger was and what to do if it happened to me, that did nothing to dissipate how often it occurred. For years I lived in a world where at any moment I might be blindsided and incapacitated by my emotions. It wasn't enough anymore to know how to treat these symptoms; I wanted to heal the cause. I wanted to understand *what causes a trigger in the first place.*

I'd been looking at the whole situation backward. I kept trying to figure out why I would get so thrown off and feel totally out of control. In actuality, in those triggered moments and the resulting aftermath, I wasn't in control. A younger version of me was.

The way I've come to understand it: as children, we experience trauma (a lasting emotional response to a stressful event) any time we encounter a situation that we were too young to process fully. Our little psyche isn't capable of handling what it's experiencing, so it fractures, splintering off. That little piece of us stays stuck in time, trapped at whatever age "they" experienced the trauma. Then that little fractured piece of you that's three years old or seventeen or twenty-two? "They" become hypervigilant—on the lookout for anything that feels like the scary thing that created them in the first place.

When you encounter something that *feels like that thing*—and of course you will at some point—that younger version of you is, unfortunately, going to freak the hell out.

To "protect" itself, it can hijack your entire system and use whatever modality it has to keep you "safe." *And* since you've lived through all kinds of hard things in your life, you've likely got all sorts of different "pieces" with totally different triggers attached to them.

It took a session with my therapist to realize why that particular phone call I mentioned set me off. The call was with an older man, and his job gave him an authoritative role—he reminded me a lot of my father. When he sounded stern, I heard anger—and when I was little, if an older male was angry, I was no longer safe. I started that phone call as a thirty-five-year-old and ended it as a frightened toddler at the wheel. The toddler? She only has the emotional skills and resources of the age she's frozen at—the only thing she knew how to do was have a meltdown.

Younger versions of us show up and make themselves known in all kinds of ways. Sometimes it's through mania or sadness or rage. Sometimes it takes form in our body through pain, illness, or disease. Sometimes it manifests as debilitating fear or the need to numb ourselves so we feel nothing at all.

It wasn't until I discovered inner-child work and internal family systems therapy (IFS), in particular, that I tried a loving approach for the first time. IFS encourages you to look at each piece and part of yourself (all those younger versions of you) with love and compassion. The quintessential book on the subject is, aptly titled, *No Bad Parts*.

Instead of getting angry, I allowed myself to feel my feelings without judgment. I worked with an energy healer who specialized in childhood trauma. She taught me to get quiet, to go inside and imagine myself talking to that feeling. The first question was always to ask that feeling how old it was.

It's startling how fast you get an answer.

I swear it feels like every age of me has shown up through this process. I've remembered so many things I'd never marked as painful until I looked at them through the eyes of an adult. It's made me hyperaware of how often children are asked to ignore their own fears and pain because they're inconvenient to adults.

Asking which version of you took over in a certain situation is crucial in understanding how to get past emotional roadblocks. It's not the twenty-seven-year-old you who shuts down during confrontation and doesn't know how to stand up for himself—it's the ten-year-old you who was taught *how he must behave* in order to receive his father's love. The anxiety you feel in the pit of your stomach whenever you see a contemporary succeeding, the same feeling that makes you self-sabotage, might be the eleven-year-old who never felt good enough.

When you realize that it's basically a five-year-old running the show it (hopefully) allows you to have some compassion for yourself. It also (hopefully) makes you realize that you don't want a five-year-old running the show. And it's much easier than you'd think to effect change.

We can do it right now if you'd like to try. Think of something uncomfortable you went through between the ages of five and ten years old. The age is totally arbitrary; I'm only mentioning it to give you some guardrails. The memory doesn't need to be deeply traumatic; in fact, it's probably best to start with something small. Search your mind until you find any experience that feels bad, and then focus in on how old you were when that happened. The memory that sprang to mind for me is from when I was eight years old, so I'm going to close my eyes and really focus in on her. I imagine exactly what I looked like at that age, where I was when it happened, what I was wearing, what was going on in my life at that moment. Then I imagine myself today, at forty-one years old, speaking to myself at eight years old.

First, I ask her what she needs from me. Over the years I've gotten every kind of response: very young versions of me often ask to be held or rocked in my grandma's old rocking chair. They've asked me to play in the park—or simply watch over them so they feel safe to play in the park. We've cuddled up to watch a movie. In fact, there's an ultracozy living room somewhere in my heart where various ages of myself are safe and warm and watching Disney's *Beauty and the Beast*. A twenty-four-year-old version of me—an exhausted new mother—just wanted someone to hold the baby so she could take a shower and put on clean clothes.

This eight-year-old version who came to mind today? She was embarrassed at school; she just wants a hug.

The next thing I ask is what she needs to tell me. This eight-year-old girl shows me how overwhelming her life is. She shows me how Mama stays in bed and how Daddy moved out. She shows me the hand-me-down tank top she wore to school, the one that was a bit too big. She shows me how she found out at the end of the day, too late to do anything, that the boys could see her little breasts through the arm holes. She was so embarrassed but didn't tell anyone what happened—there was no one who would care. At least that's what it felt like to her.

I care, I tell her. I hold that little girl and let her say everything she needs to. We have the conversation I would have with my own daughter if the same thing happened today. I ask her if there's anything else she needs. *A different shirt*, she says. A simple white T-shirt. Something nobody can peek through. This one is brand new, not a hand-me-down. She puts it on. She feels so much better.

I take her to the sofa, the one filled with safe, happy versions of me snuggled in together. It's the scene where Belle is singing about the village—that's our favorite part.

The last thing I do in these imaginings is ask myself (who I am today) if there's something I needed to see when I was that younger version of myself. When it feels right, I take myself on a tour of some relevant part of my life today. I often show the little girl me, so desperate for affection from her parents, the loving relationship I have with my own children. I'll show the eighteen-year-old who lives paycheck to paycheck and is crying over how she'll pay rent the balance on my savings account so she knows that we're safe now. I show thirty-seven-year-old me, who's lost inside a hideous divorce, what my life looks like today inside of a healthy, loving relationship with a good man.

This gentle visualization is the most effective form of self-therapy I have ever discovered. I know it works because I can feel an almost instantaneous drop in the intense emotion the memory brought up. And once I do this healing work with these pieces of me, I am never triggered by them again. That's not to say I'm never triggered at all—there's a lot of memories to work through, especially for those of us with difficult pasts. But I'm never haunted by the same memory again. I believe this happens because on some level, when we reimagine what *should have* happened to that version of us, our current selves help our past selves heal.

I've worked with this idea of my current self, helping my younger self, for the past few years. In that time, I've experienced the most profound healing of my life—but will you allow me to take this just a little further? To this cosmic sort of question that's been swirling around in my head for months??

If our current self can help our past self heal . . . then couldn't our future self help our current self too? This is definitely too deep of a topic for me to just toss out here at the end of a chapter—though *my goodness*, if we ever find ourselves around a campfire sipping out of enamel mugs and discussing the universe, I would absolutely adore a deep discussion of nonlinear time theory with you. But for now, let's just call this an exercise in imagination and consider this: Imagine yourself twenty years in the future as the best possible version of you. If you lived the next twenty years with as much health and vitality and love as you were able to—***this*** vision is who you would be.

Now . . . what does that version of you know that current you might not? What do you worry about today that *that* version of you doesn't concern themselves with at all? What would that version of you say if they were sitting with you right now? I go to the sixty-year-old version of myself for advice all the time. She comes with me on long runs and lays out her mat next to mine at yoga class. That's the mentor who reminds me to slow down when I'm with my kids. She reminds me to savor a long kiss with my love. She agrees to read my daughter another story at bedtime. I tend to push and force and try to hurry things along . . . but not sixty-year-old me; she's chill, she's vibing, she's very, very calm. After a lifetime of accidentally letting my younger, wounded selves run things, I'm aiming to allow my older, wiser, *healed* self to lead from here on out.

~~How~~ Who are you feeling?

What is it with families and guilt?

How do they know *exactly* the right thing to say to make you feel like a million tons of crap in order to get you to fall in line? No, *you don't* want to take three Spirit Airlines flights *and a nine-hour Greyhound bus trip* to attend your second cousin's baby's baptism. You don't want to, but you probably will. Sometimes it's just easier than enduring the drama.

Or maybe this time you put your foot down—you hold firm and refuse to cave. But now you're being eaten alive by anxiety because you've made your parent/auntie/grandfather (or the whole lot of them!) angry.

They're not mad, they say; they're just "disappointed." Barf.

In case you've never talked it through with your therapist, *this* little scenario is called **emotional manipulation**. That's when *someone else* tries to control, affect, or even exploit *your emotions* to get you to do what they want you to do. The reason your family is so damn good at emotional manipulation is because they've known you all your life—they have years of practice.

There's an old joke David Foster Wallace once told about two young fish who are swimming in the ocean. An older fish swims by and says, "Morning, boys. How's the water?"

The two young fish swim on for a bit before one looks at the other in total confusion: "What the hell is water?"

Your family is the water you grew up in, and since it's always been around you, it's highly possible you don't even know it exists.

The "water" in my extended family? So toxic, it's a wonder we don't all have third eyes and superpowers. In the course of my adult life, I've broken up with a lot of family members rather than stay in the toxicity with them.

Perhaps it's inaccurate to say "a lot."

A handful? A smattering?

The point is, more than once I've come to the realization that I don't want to keep someone hateful in my life just because we share DNA.

Sometimes when I tell people that I have family members I don't speak to anymore, they're flabbergasted. Their family would *never*. They come from lineage or cultures—Italians, Irish, Kardashian—where everyone sticks together, no matter what. They grew up in tight-knit groups. Their people might be crazy, but "family is family."

It doesn't matter that your aunt Janice slept with your college boyfriend over the Thanksgiving holiday. Aunt Janice is family, and you *will* encounter that deceitful troll at every christening and Fourth of July BBQ from now until forever.

Not I, says the cat.

I will not do life with anyone toxic or abusive, regardless of how we're related. The only exception to this rule is obviously my children, who at times have been both *toxic* and *abusive*—as toddlers, they were often both simultaneously. Other than my kids, the only people who are allowed in my life are the good ones. I have a strict "no asshole" policy.

You can be whoever you are: quiet, loud, an oversharer, a control freak, a stoner, an ultraconservative, living in a throuple, super into keto . . . literally, I'm here for you being you. But I absolutely cannot stand the noxious energy that weaves its way through generations like a diseased branch of the family tree.

Most big families have at least one vile relative, right? There's always, like, one person somewhere between thirty-one and seventy-three who has been angry their whole life. They stir up drama between family gatherings and are easier to set off than the wires of a nuclear warhead. Everyone is mildly terrified of Aunt Brenda or Grandpa Jim or Cousin Lois. They do their best to stay out of the line of fire. A bunch of grown people making decisions based on the angry whims of one emotionally unwell matriarch? Sounds unbelievable to some, but for the vast majority, their family's version of this behavior has gone on forever, so it feels normal.

What the hell is water?

To be fair to Aunt Brenda or Grandpa Jim or your dad or your mother-in-law, the "water" they're swimming in? They didn't create it either. They're emotionally interacting with the younger generation in whatever way their elders emotionally interacted with them. So if Nana used guilt and shame in her parenting, unless your mama has done her own work, it's the only way she'll know how to interact with you. Nana used anger and fear to control her children, and your mother uses praise and passive aggression . . . but the underlying drive is the same.

If an authority figure used emotional manipulation to gain your compliance as a child, it's wired into your makeup to be predisposed to it as an adult. And here's the rub: the person manipulating you doesn't even need to be the original authority figure. If the situation reminds you—even unconsciously—of the behavior you're used to, you'll comply without even considering it. Why?

An emotional boundary is your ability to separate your feelings from someone else's. It's the understanding that *your* emotions are not tied to *their* emotions. Your mother / father-in-law / sister / bestie / husband / girlfriend / the terrifying yet beautiful grandmother from *Crazy Rich Asians* . . . however *they feel* should not affect your *feelings*.

That hasn't occurred to most of us because we were raised as an extension of those family members: if Mama was angry, we were affected. If Daddy was happy, it made us happy. Eventually we learned that how we acted could make them angry or proud. Now unless you were a different sort of creature (shout-out to the strong-willed children who refuse to conform!), you likely learned to do things to please them and avoid things that made them angry, which is why you're well into your fourth decade and find yourself on that Greyhound heading to Crystal's baby's baptism rather than tell your mother no.

And not to belabor this point, but the reason you're thinking *I am thirty-eight years old. How am I this afraid of my mother?* and yet still drowning in misery is because of the emotion attached to the thing that's overriding you. The part that's teetering on the edge of a full-blown meltdown at the idea of Mama being mad isn't the rational grown-ass woman that you are, remember?

Standing up for yourself and what you need is hard, especially if you don't have a lot of practice and particularly if the person you're standing up to has never encountered healthy interactions. Shout-out to us for going to therapy to learn to deal with all of the people in our lives who won't go to therapy!

This stuff is hard. But also walking is hard if you've never done it. Not pooping your pants is hard if you're a newbie. Driving for the first time felt wild, but somehow you figured it out. We're really good at figuring out how to do things when the payoff seems worth it, and trust me, this payoff *is* worth it.

At least for me it is.

I plan to spend the rest of my life doing my best to heal the wounds of my past, learn from the mistakes I've made, and grow into a better version of me with each passing day. That's a lot to ask of one person, and it's utterly impossible if I'm trying to do those things while simultaneously taking responsibility for the emotions of the other adults in my life.

It's not your fault that you don't have emotional boundaries and aren't sure how to put them into place . . . but once you become aware of their lack, once you have a glimpse of a way to find more personal freedom through healing, once you have the knowledge of how to get free, *it is your fault* if you stay stuck.

What the *actual* fuck?!

Has there ever been any term as functional as the f-word? It can be used to express shock, awe, fear, and fury. It can be sexy, dirty, offensive, and aggressive. The question *What the fuck?* could be used in dismay, in anger, or even as an agreement.

"Hey, you want to try bungee jumping with me?"

"*What the fuck*, let's do it!"

When I was growing up, that phrase was really only the three words, but several years back, another descriptor was added to the mix. *Actual.* I don't know why that word in particular makes for such a stronger sticking point, but it's really effective. *What the actual fuck* expresses so much more than its predecessor, and I like reserving this question for moments in life when whatever is happening is so terribly shocking, it would almost be comical if it weren't so tragic.

The first time I met my boyfriend's family was also the same day I realized I was pregnant with his baby. We had only been dating for nine months.

I already have four children.

So, you know, *super chill.*

The goddess of chaos—or whatever mythical creature is supposed to be in charge of that—must have been laughing her ass off.

I was not laughing. I was warily walking through the streets of London trying to find a pharmacy where I could procure a pregnancy test from one of those unmanned checkout machines. I bought what I needed plus a book of sudoku puzzles I never planned on solving, just to have something to hide the test underneath.

Back in the hotel room, I peed on the stick and then just sat there in stunned silence staring at the instantaneous results. When you're *trying* to get pregnant, those tests take forever to give you an answer. When you're trying *not* to get pregnant, that wand lights up like the Rockefeller Center Christmas Tree the second a single droplet touches it.

The thing is, I knew what that test was going to show long before I walked into Boots to buy it. This was not my first rodeo. My boobs were big, my pants were way too tight, and my period was MIA. The test was really just confirmation—but that confirmation was terrifying. *What was I going to do? How would I tell him? What would my kids think? What would my Mema think? How would this affect my career? Can you breastfeed with implants?* All sorts of supremely unhelpful thoughts crashed into one another inside my mind, an energy field ripe for panic.

Here's the thing about me though . . . **I'm incredible in a crisis**.

If your house burns down . . . or your girlfriend cheats on you with your mom . . . or your company is about to tank after another bad quarter—I'm your Huckleberry.

The moment in that hotel bathroom was exactly that—a moment.

I don't ease into things. I don't take time to marinate in the possible change.

I accept what is, I choose a new direction, and *I go*.

Some people approach big life transitions with the precision of a brain surgeon's scalpel. I approach things with the grace of a meat cleaver.

I learned a long time ago that life will take a wild left turn when you least expect it. You can take the time to ponder how it happened and debate the reasons why and go through all the stages—and that's likely a healthier approach—but for me, that's only delaying the inevitable.

Eventually, you're going to have to accept whatever your new reality is. You'll need to make the best of it. So I typically skip the shock and awe and just get on with it.

So my brain flipped from *Holy f*ck balls, what the actual sh%t? How in the name of all that is . . .*

To *OK, I'm going to have a baby, and, yes, having five kids will be a challenge, but my kids are the greatest thing that's ever happened to me, even if they're monsters sometimes, and this will be fine. Clearly this baby was meant to be here, and if it's meant to be here, then I will have whatever skills I need to love it well. Amen.*

I really do accept things that quickly. It doesn't mean I won't unpack it and pick it apart later, but it does mean that almost immediately, I give myself some new direction to head in. Once I'm walking down a new path, it's easier for me to find some positives to cling to.

There was only one problem with my new plan: my partner didn't ever plan on having children. He never planned on having kids, and at only nine months in, he was still trying to wrap his brain around the fact that he was in love with a woman who had four of them. Plus, loving *someone else's* children who are capable of sleeping through the night and wiping their own butt *is very different* than having your own newborn. It was a lot of change in a short amount of time for someone who'd never been a husband or a father.

But, you'll recall, I'd already accepted this new reality, and as much as I knew he'd be surprised by the news, I also knew he would be the most amazing dad ever. He is so unfailingly caring and thoughtful. He is calm beyond reason—a cool mountain lake of peace to quench my fiery, intense lava bubbling just below the surface. We're a beautiful balance for each other, and I had total confidence in us.

I anticipated that he would be shocked, because same.

What I *didn't* anticipate was that he would be upset, disappointed, and terrified.

I'd never told someone I was pregnant and had it met with anything but positivity—I had no idea what a privilege that was. He was so loving and supportive of me, but the baby only generated fear. And he wasn't the only one.

From my best friends to my family members, everyone met the news with shock, followed closely by a *oh-shit-you're-gonna-have-five-kids*. It was like telling someone you've decided to undergo surgery to have a third boob added to your chest.

With each passing week, I felt more and more alone. I grew increasingly paranoid that other people's negativity would affect the baby, and so I started to avoid everyone. I didn't want to have to try to keep convincing people that this must be meant to be. I started to wonder if I might have to raise this baby on my own.

In retrospect, it was extremely unfair to ask someone else—particularly someone who had no experience with parenting—to adjust to the idea as quickly as I had. As time passed, he began to, very nervously, get excited. He started buying little gifts for the baby, board books in black and white because he'd read that she wouldn't be able to see color at the beginning. He obsessed over the prenatal vitamin I was taking and did ridiculous amounts of research to ensure I had the best available.

After a few months, the initial shock had worn off, and in its place was nervous anticipation and a belly that was getting too big for my stretchy pants. I won't say that we were both totally at peace with what was coming, but we were totally aligned with our ability to take it on together.

At the start of my fourth month, we went to the doctor for a routine checkup. As soon as the wand touched my body, I felt the energy in my OB shift. The doctor asked the nurse to turn the lights down in the room because she was having a hard time seeing the screen. In all my pregnancies, I've never had a doctor say she couldn't see the screen. My heart began to beat so hard, I thought it would break through my chest. She kept dragging that ultrasound wand all around my uterus, and my boyfriend was squeezing my hand so hard, it hurt—he knew something was wrong too.

"I'm so sorry, Rachel. The baby doesn't have a heartbeat."

What came next was . . . horrendous.

My baby was dead—but my body didn't know it. I hadn't had a miscarriage because my body wouldn't let go. It remained pregnant, doing everything in its power to keep the baby safe long after there was a reason to do so.

The doctor told me she could perform a procedure, or an inexpensive medicine from the grocery store pharmacy would allow me to go through the process at home. Either way I had to decide quickly. They didn't know how long I'd been like this, and too much time could be dangerous for me.

I thought I'd been knocked down in just about every way I could be, but lying in bed while your body saves itself by washing away your baby is a unique kind of hell. I've never experienced something so profoundly horrible. On some level, I felt like I'd failed at my most important job: keeping my child safe.

I know that's not true. I know my body and the baby's body did the best that they could. I know that sometimes these things happen. I know that it's common.

But knowing something in your brain does very little for the pain you feel in your heart. That particular pain? It was the final straw. I'd spent the previous two years surviving one wave of pain after another. I could no longer keep my head above water. I was lost at sea.

Something I couldn't have known before having a miscarriage is how hard it is to navigate the grief of the experience when nobody else—no matter how supportive or loving—seems to understand how you feel. Worse still is continuing to grieve one month, two months, six months later, and the people that love you most look at you helplessly, wondering, *Why isn't she over this yet?*

Why in the world would all of this happen? Why push my partner from terror to excitement, only to have that dream ripped away? In fact, why give me the vision of this baby at all if it wasn't meant to be here??

I live my life looking for meaning in everything that happens, but I truly couldn't find any here. I had an obsessive need to make sense of what had happened. Because it didn't make any sense at all.

I wasn't at all rational. I kept circling this idea that maybe I *was* supposed to have another baby and I needed to prove to God or the universe that I wanted it enough to try again. One night when I was particularly hormonal, I asked my partner—the one who had held me all night long as I bled our baby out onto giant pads stacked one on top of another—I asked him if he thought we were supposed to try again.

"No, darling," he told me very softly, "I don't."

Whatever semblance of sanity I had been holding onto shattered. I wept and sobbed and tried to argue.

"But *why*—why would this happen if it wasn't a sign?"

"Rachel, if you hadn't gotten pregnant, would you have ever considered having another child?"

"No, but, but . . . things don't just happen like this without—"

"Things *do just happen like this*. All the time. Sometimes awful things just happen. That's life. It's beautiful that you want to find meaning in it. But sometimes you have to accept that it's hard or unfair or total shit. Maybe the meaning you take away is that you survived—that we survived it together—and that's pretty beautiful all on its own."

Shit happens.

It's a bumper sticker for a reason.

Some days you're a vintage Porsche roadster driving down PCH on a perfect summer evening. Other days you're the little butterfly who's flapping around, enjoying your day, and you slam headfirst into the windshield of the sports car that's winding its way up the coast. I don't know why life is that way *but it is*.

Years ago, I read *Tiny Beautiful Things* by Cheryl Strayed. I don't want to be like a hipster talking about the hottest pizza place in town . . . but I liked that thing before it was cool.

The book is a collection of advice that Cheryl gave to people who sent letters asking for help. That entire book is basically a miracle of wisdom. I truly think it should be required reading for every human on the planet. But there's this one line in particular that I have never, ever forgotten. In bed that night, lost in painful confusion and uncertainty, that line came back to me again.

A man sent a letter in, writing in sum total, essentially, "What the fuck?"

And Cheryl wrote back the most profound reply: *"The 'fuck' is your life."*

This is **all** our life.

The good stuff, the hard stuff, the absolute shit . . . **it's all our life**. When you get a promotion, when you get fired, when the dog runs away or your long-lost lover returns . . . **it's all your**

life. When your career is on top, when you screw up royally, when you're bored out of your skull . . . **it's all your life**. When you fall in love again, when your father dies, when your daughter tells you you're mean, when your son fills your name in on his college application under the question "Who's your hero?" . . . **it's all your life**.

My baby died.

And in the aftermath of grief, I latched onto the idea that *this* must be the end of enduring such painful experiences. After all, I've had a lot of awful things happen in my life and endured enough trauma to fill a book (many of them, as it so happens). And not that this is a competition, but sometimes I look around at other people's lives and stories, and I can't comprehend how their path can be so different from mine.

When the baby died and I had to push pills up inside my body that caused me to hemorrhage her out, I went a little crazy. What I latched onto was this: *It can't get worse than this. This is the most awful it will ever be.*

But that's untrue.

That's the kind of thing you say to yourself to try to cope with intense pain—*at least it won't be this bad again.*

But then, a year later, my children's father died suddenly. We were utterly blindsided. Every second of those days was overwhelming, broken up only by small pockets of time where overwhelm swung to horror and back again.

I had to help my children pick out the clothes we'd bury their father in. I had to go through the closet of my ex-husband to gather his favorite jeans, still slung over the cabinet from the last time he'd taken them off. I stared into his sock drawer in bewilderment: *When someone dies, are you supposed to bury them with socks on?* We'd chosen his favorite sneakers, and in life, you'd obviously wear those with socks, but did it matter now? Of all the horrible things we walked through in the aftermath of his death, I cannot explain to you how much choosing socks for him to be buried in destroyed me.

Me, standing at the sock drawer? That's my life too.

When I began writing to you, I wanted to focus on the questions that helped me change my life for the better—but it strikes me now that this particular question is the only rhetorical one of the bunch. It's more statement than question, more expletive than request. Sometimes you just need something to scream at the heavens, and this question works as well as any despite the fact that you're not likely to get an answer. There's no real answer. I'm including it anyway because I hope to shift your perception of this question and the circumstances that might prompt your using it.

When things are working in a way we like, when life is good, it's easy to think, *Man, this is living!* When things go "wrong," we hope it's just a momentary pause in this majestic thing we call our life.

But life is all of it.

It's not about living for the parts that are good and numbing out the pieces that suck. It's about making peace with the fact that you will experience both.